SEE ME FOR WHO I AM

Graham Culton

SEE ME FOR WHO I AM

Graham Culton

ISBN 978-1-914615-34-4

A CIP catalogue record for this

book is available from the British Library.

Published 2022 Tricorn Books, Aspex

42 The Vulcan Building Gunwharf Quays
Portsmouth PO1 3BF

SEE ME FOR WHO I AM

A Percentage of the profits from

SEE ME FOR WHO I AM

Will go to the Charity

Talking to Minds

http://www.talking2minds.co.uk/

CONTENTS

ACKNOWLEDGEMENTS	6
SEE ME FOR WHO I AM	14
INFANCY	16
THE MOVE – A NEW START	23
ALNESS ACADEMY YEARS	38
COLLEGE AND TA SERVICE	46
ENLISTMENT INTO 1ST BATTALION QUEEN'S OWN HIGHLANDERS	63
PHASE TWO INFANTRY TRAINING	86
THE CLAN	99
NORTHERN IRELAND	113
CAREER SUMMARY	117
DIARY OF EVENTS	127
FOR EVERY ACTION – THERE WILL ALWAYS BE A REACTION!	139
POSITIVE PROACTIVE ACTION	157

Acknowledgements

For far too long throughout my own personal life journey, I have been encased in a society of 'Hatred – Sorrow – Heartache – Guilt – Manipulation – Intimidation – Greed – Empowerment – Belittlement', as well as a wide 'Array of Abuse'.
Yet… at the same time, I have been surrounded by Pure and Positive Beauty – Love – Compassion – Honest – Dignified and Loyal Trustworthy Individuals.
I have been blinded from so much 'Positivity' by the darkness of 'Negativity'.
I have been tirelessly in search of 'Empathy' throughout my own life journey.
Sympathy is NOT what I have been seeking from birth to the here and now.
Having my own personal understanding and positive realisation of much, has truly and positively enabled myself to move/progress forwards in life, in a much more positive and pro-active manner of panache.

'I Love Who I am, and What I Do in Life'

It seems that it takes for myself to hit 'Crisis Point' in order for myself to see aspects of life in a more positive perspective!

During my last week employed as a Fire Marshal Manager at the London 2012 Olympic Games at Woolwich Barracks, I ventured out around the venue in order to check up on the guys (marshals). The lads managed to have their photo taken with Team GB's Peter Wilson, who won Gold in the double-trap shotgun event. I was fortunate to witness Peter qualify for the final, as well as experience the treble-A-moment, when Peter knew he had become a World Olympic Hero. Seeing Peter standing on the winners' podium, with the iconic *Chariots of Fire* theme tune playing, followed by the British National Anthem, and seeing the Union flag being raised in unison with the National Anthem, will forever remain in my Memorable moments in life for eternity.

During my last twenty minutes of shift at Woolwich Barracks, I went for a walk down past the Finals Hall, towards the shotgun range. In the distance, I saw a Team GB athlete walking towards me!

Only turned out to be Peter Wilson. Peter offered his hand to me, and before I could say anything, he thanked me! I was somewhat overwhelmed with Peter's positive gesture. When my moment of speechlessness had evaporated, I asked Peter if I could have my photo taken with him. He gladly obliged, prior to taking his Gold medal out of his rucksack. I was surprisingly shocked that Peter wanted to put his medal around my neck for the purpose of the positive pictorial. Peter informed me that earlier on in the day, the other marshals had enlightened him, that I was an Armed Forces Veteran and that was why he had thanked me before.

I was on a day off, come the day of the Opening Ceremony of the Paralympic Games. I felt somewhat out of routine that day! So much so, that I enquired whether I could work at the ceremony. The answer was yes.

I met some truly amazing and inspirational individuals/ friends during both my time at the Olympics and Paralympic Games, from where I witnessed sheer determination and passion and much admired courage by many individuals, especially the Paralympian Athletes.

Questions I have continually asked myself time and time again…

1) Why do I still find struggles in life?
2) How is it humanely possible that I could have had so many achievements in life, throughout my 39-year-life journey… through events that I have experienced from birth to the here and now. Including… heartache – Sorrow – Grief – Physical and Mental Anguish/Adversity ?

Only answers that I can give myself! I have achieved all that I have through having positive focus and determination to overcome unknown difficulties encountered during my 39-year-journey.

'Now I Feel Loved'

At times… I have felt Lovelorn, with My Heart Torn!
Now I feel Loved and Respected by Many 'GrayT Individuals'.
Now I feel Love and Affection – from All around the World.
At times… I have felt somewhat 'Maladjusted'!
Now I feel positively Lusted.
As long as You are with Me… There's No Place I'd rather Be!
'Heaven is a Place on Earth' – Belinda Carlisle. X
Love is an 'Eternal Flame' – The Bangles. X
I Love You All – My Treble-A-fb-Family – 'Truly-Madly-Deeply – Savage Garden.
'Always and Forever' – Luther Vandross.
I shall never ever be 'Alone' – Heart. X

Throughout Life from Here on in… THANK YOU (Dido).
X
Love – Hugs – Respect – Regards and Forever Positive Friendship.

Gray. xoxoxoxoxoxox
'Who I Am'

I am a Son – A Father – I am also a Brother.
I have done Many a GrayT – Deed in Life… including being a Lover.
I am a Nephew – A Cousin, I am also a 'GrayT Friend Indeed'.
I am also a 'Positive Member of Humanity'… Of this Fact… Many – I'm Sure can and will Verify.
I've been a Baker – A Soldier – A GrayT Friend in Life.
I've once been Married to a 'Beautiful Wife'.
I have Lived a 39-Year-Life', enshrouded by 'Erratic Mystery'!
I have Lived a Life full of 'Positive GrayT Opportunities'.
At the same time – A Life Darkened by Negativity – Anguish and Adversity!
'Who I Am'. Graham Robert Culton.

I would love to pay honourable and respectable homage to the following 'GrayT and Loving Individuals'.
Bill, Jenny, David and Bonnie Tatnall, Debs and Kelly, Billy and Tracey, Dan and Amy, Chris and Paula Dragun and family, Dougie, Carol and Kris Culton, Lynn McNamee and Family, 'Lt Colonel C. Lockhart', Andy and Jo Priaulx and family, Condor Ferries, Dame Vera Lyn and family, Dame Esther Rantzen, Sir Chris Hoy, Graeme Obree (The Flying Scotsman), The Mighty-Mo Farrah and family, David Weir

(Weirwolf), Ellie Symmonds, Matt Le Tissier, Anton Du Becke, Cilla Black, Rula Lenska, The Not Forgotten Association, The Royal British Legion, Talking2Minds, Veterans-In-Action, Remount, The Warrior Programme, Dave Player @ Kartforce (Respect+ Regards Mucker), Snow Patrol for helping me to discover both the word 'EMPATHY' and Your Treble-A-Music, James Vine and Theo Morgan, Danni and Brad Ogier, Steph Lyons and family, Debs and Shola Cook, Peter Wilson, Vice Admiral Sir John Francis Coward KCB DSO, Sports Direct Crew – Guernsey – Simon Leyman, Rose+Nikki Cutler, Jared Roland, Ben Wilen, David Haimes, Richard Mahy, Jordan Burtenshaw, Scott Brouard,. Janet and Chris Palmer (Wiltshire), Bournemouth Church's Housing Association – St Paul's Night Shelter, Robbie Williams and family, Amanda Benell, Inars Renckulbergs, Russ and Ley Roberts and family (A True Friendship that Will Never Fail), James, Zoe, Cayleigh @ 'WALKABOUT' – Cardiff, Becky Clark (Aldershot), Jim Davidson – comedian, John Nettles – (Jim! – John – Barnaby!), Miley Cyrus and family X, Jade Thirwall and 'Little Mix Lovelies', Mica Paris, Guernsey Welfare Service, Reverend Graeme Beebee and Congregation from the Church of Scotland – St Peter Port Guernsey, Craig Howie, Wee Craig, Kate, Jay Rogers, Tommy Wylie, Clesio, Ivo, Manuel, Miguel, Jeff, and everyone @ 'CT Guernsey',

Simon and Theo Scott (Salisbury), Dame Mary and Doug Perkins and family and all staff @ Specsavers, Jason Savident, Chris Williamson, Stu Allan, Robbie Dover, Gary (Alba), Mick Dorey and Family, Neil Marsh and family, Tony Marchant and family and Staff @ Folies Nightclub, Tanya and Chris Jackson and family, Eric Quintal and Everyone @ Vodafone (Guernsey), Christopher Biggins, Russ Abbot, Chico, Debbie McGee, James Martin (Chef), Tiffany Hill, Madeleine Russel and family, and to 'Each and Every Member of My Treble-A-fb-Family', and to All of the Lovely Ladies and GrayT Guys that I have met in 'Costa Coffee shops in Congleton – Hanley – Crewe – Macclesfield.

And finally… I would just love to say a MASSIVE THANK YOU to the following: Andy Cook and Louise Stones, Chris Bovaird, Martin Lawes + Derek the DAWG, Elliot Holman, Donna Alos, Chris Best, Travis Mitchell, NICKSY, James Everton, Pat Sharp (the PatMan), Sara Hartill, Jaunty, Gail, Jenny, Management and SalesLovelies @ Signal 1. No 1 for Staffordshire and Cheshire. Each and everyone involved/ associated with Heart FM all regions, BBC Radio 1 and 2 and 5 Live, Silk FM. I am finally paying mutual and positive sentiments (as above) to all the many-many-great and positive friends that I have befriended throughout my 39-year life journey. The Journey Continues… Onwards and Upwards.

As I come to the end of one chapter in life and prepare for the next Chapter!
I am throwing Up a MASSIVE SALUTE to Her Majesty the Queen and all members of HM Royal Family, each and every member of HM Armed Forces (past and present). We will remember all those, who have made the Ultimate Sacrifice' in the name of HM Queen and Country.

PS NEVER JUDGE A BOOK by its COVER.
Please be Intrigued…!
Be Happy.
Be Positive.
Be Yourself.
Be Loved.
Cheers aye, Gray. xoxoxoxoxoxoxoxoxox

PLEASE DON'T LOOK AT ME DIFFERENTLY!
I ONLY ACCEPT SUPPORT AND EMPATHY.

MANY A PLACE I HAVE BEEN,
TOO MANY HORRORS I HAVE SEEN.

ON MANY ROADS, I'VE MET MANY JUNCTIONS
NEVER UNDERSTANDING MY PSYCHOLOGICAL
FUNCTIONS.

FOR "QUEEN AND COUNTRY" – I WAS LOYAL,
AT THE BEST OF TIMES – MY HEAD FILLED
WITH TRAUMATIC TURMOIL!

I FIND IT HARD TO LEAVE MY TROUBLES
BEHIND.
ALL THIS LEAVES ME WITH A TROUBLED MIND!

I SHARE MY PAIN WITH MY BROTHERS AND
SISTERS IN ARMS.
EQUALLY – WE ALL HAVE OUR DISTINCTIVE
ALARMS.

MY COLOURS – THEY WERE GREEN AND
BROWN!
FROM THE DAY I GAVE MY OATH OF
ALLEGIANCE TO THE CROWN.

SEE ME FOR WHO I AM

GRAHAM CULTON
DISABLED ARMED FORCES VETERAN
12/10/09

I wrote this poem whilst in Albecq Wards (CMH-Hospital) Guernsey in 2009, having been diagnosed with post-traumatic stress disorder. I was enabled to transform 'negative thoughts' in my mind – onto paper in a positive manner – to share with many others. I was listening to Snow Patrol's 'Chasing Cars' at the time of writing. Respect to Snow Patrol.

Saturday 9th March 2013

SEE ME FOR WHO I AM

My name is Graham Robert Culton. I am a 38-year-old Armed Forces Veteran of ten and a half years service to Queen and Country. I served with Mortar Platoon of 2nd Battalion – 51st Highland Volunteers in Dingwall (in the Highlands) for a year prior to giving my Oath of Allegiance to Queen and Country and proudly joining the 1st Battalion – Queen's Own Highlanders (the 'Blue Maff') Caber Feigh Gu Braith in 1993.

I was born on the 25th January 1975 (Robert Burns day – famous Scottish poet). I was born in the Eastern General Hospital in Edinburgh. My parents were Raymond Douglas and Fiona Margo Culton. My Dad was a 22-year Royal Navy – Falklands Veteran F-90 (frigate) HMS *Brilliant*. I am aware that he also served on board F-72 HMS *Ariadne*. My mum was a housewife. I have an older sister – Margaret – who works for the NHS in Dundee, and is married to Andy Moir. I also have a stepbrother and sister through my dad's second marriage to Sue. Steven and Nicola are their names.

See Me For Who I Am is my life story from birth to present. This is my journey/voyage in life, involving aspects of a) my childhood, b) education, c) family lifestyle, d) career, and e) challenges and positive life experiences. My story will include black humour (Army talk for laughter/banter). Heartache and sorrow. Positive and negative events along my route in life. Most of all the book shall be filled with empathy for many. The book will also include some great and awesome friendships – camaraderie. I will endeavour to create simplicity and understanding for all that choose to read/share my journey.

Cheers aye, Gray

Everybody wants Happiness – Nobody wants Pain!
You Can't have a Rainbow….Without a Little Rain.

Anon.

INFANCY

I do not have a great deal of recollection of my early development years in life, as from birth my journey in life was only beginning. I am unable to pinpoint accurately my world of self-discovery. I will endeavour to give an accurate and honest (sincere) account of events as they occurred to the best of my ability.

I vaguely remember being brought up at 70 Teandallon Place in Evanton, Ross-shire. I was the only male in the house. My mum and dad got divorced at an age that I was too young to understand what divorce meant (age two). Through my dad's service to Queen and Country in the Royal Navy, my sister Margaret was born in Hong Kong.

When Margaret Thatcher was prime minister in 1982, and the decree was given to deploy the Task Force down to the South Atlantic, after the invasion of the Falkland Islands by Argentinian Forces, I was none the wiser in knowing that my dad (my hero) was one of the many brave souls involved.

I remember being out in the park, in front of the house during the Falklands. I also remember that we had snow, and I (like most kids) was out enjoying the moment of building snowmen and snowball fights with friends.

I was one of the lucky kids, to have my dad come back alive. Other kids were not so lucky. My sincere thoughts and prayers forever go out to those families – Now – Forever –

Always. I always have those many families in my thoughts come Remembrance Sunday. And I always endeavour to get out booted and suited with my medals and a copy of my dad's South Atlantic Medal, which I wear in both respect and fond and loving memory of my dad – Raymond (Rocky) Culton. I always wear the South Atlantic medal on the right breast of my suit jacket.

Other than my sister Margaret and myself, I have a small level of knowledge that there would have been a third child in the Evanton address. My mum was, like all mums, Loving – Caring – Sharing and Friendly. My mum, Fiona, experienced her first episode of mental ill health following the loss of a third Culton child at birth. My mum was affected by postnatal depression following this life-changing traumatic event.

My mum spent much of her time as a single mother, in and out of mental health hospital, which in turn led to Margaret and myself leading unstable lifestyles, in and out of child/ foster care. I have one vivid recollection of one individual foster family, where I believe Margaret and I were subject to cruel psychological abuse. On another occasion, Margaret and I were separated and I was placed in the care and support of a loving family. That loving family were the Munros.

My presence in their care obviously brought about changes in their individual lifestyles. Changes that we were all able to adapt to in no time. The last time I saw Ross was during my last year with the Highlanders, whilst based at Redford Infantry Barracks in Edinburgh, in 2002.

It was brilliant meeting up with Ross; we were able to have a catch-up. Ross was serving with the Royal Scots Dragoon Guard's Pipes and Drums. One hundred per cent admirable respect to both Ross and his regiment. I truly appreciate pipes and drums music. The RSDG's *Braveheart* theme and 'Gael' are my favourite tunes by the lads. Cheers aye, Gray.

Braveheart is one of my all-time favourite movies with awesome actors/actresses. Stephen the mad Irishman is superb in his role. Not bad for a Scotsman! The movie also portrays the history of the William Wallace era in a positive and captivating manner. Admirable respect and admiration to everyone involved with the treble-A film. Absolutely – Awesome – Amazing.

The first school that I attended was Kiltearn Primary in Evanton. I have a fond memory of walking to school in the mornings, and most mornings there was a massive HGV lorry that passed by. The cab was fitted with airhorns, and I always used to signal to the driver to blow the horns – respect to his good self, always got a couple of honks.

I remember during one term, the school had an entertainment show put on. It was a show that all pupils were asked to contribute a couple of pounds towards. I never got to see the show as I spent the money on football stickers. My punishment for my wrongdoing was to sit in the classroom in isolation. Ah well… at least I managed to get some decent stickers for my football album.

During residence at 70 Teandallon Place, my sister got a golden labrador puppy; she named him Duke. Margaret was all excited when she got home. She took Duke up to her room and before long, came running back downstairs hysterically screaming to my mum that Duke had left his trademark on her bed! I was laughing hysterically at both Duke's deed of marking his territory as well as my sister's hysterical mannerisms! Sorry Mags… nae offence intended.

One well disclosed memory of which I fondly hold from childhood was one when I believe I experienced a minor case of 'Skiveritis' (not an actual term). I woke one morning for school. I decided to rub my forehead with the palms of my hands and in doing this act, I gave my mum the impression that I had a temperature! Result! The palm trick worked and my mum told me to stay at home for the day.

I then went down to the living room and switched on the TV in time for *Sesame Street* starting. During the programme, I enjoyed all of the characters – Big Bird, Oscar the Grouch, Bert and Ernie (Trevor Jeffries and myself) LOL. Trevor is a fellow veteran friend that I met whilst residing at Mike Jackson House in Aldershot, Hampshire in 2010.

*MJH is a supported housing project for homeless/vulnerable Armed Forces veterans. It is managed by the English Church Housing Group. The house was named after General Sir Mike Jackson. Admirable respect to your good self sir. Cheers aye, Gray.

Mike Jackson House offers 25 self-contained flats to single veterans. I class MJH as a safe haven as well as a stepping stone for single veterans to enable them to get their lives back on track in a positive and professional manner, with support and guidance from an awesome management and support team and structure. Much thanks and true appreciation to all the following: ALL management, Chris, Jane, Jo, Hazel, Anne, Lawrie, Shanie, Anita, Mary and all staff. Cheers aye, Gray.

Getting back to *Sesame Street* (not forgetting Cookie Monster and Mr Snuffulufukuss – Snuffie, as I always called him). All the characters were getting ready to jet off on holiday. The one particular memory I have from that episode was what I believe to be my first experience of emotional sadness! This came about once all of the characters had boarded the plane! Well – all except for one individual – Snuffie – was left stood alone and isolated on the airport apron. I expressed tears of sadness at Snuffie's isolation once the plane had taken off.

I first shared this memory on Facebook on Wednesday 10th October 2012. Coincidentally, this date is World Mental Health Day.

This memory was shared with a fellow veteran friend and brother in arms, as well as fellow Jock fae Edinburgh – Andrew Bennett. Admirable respect and forever friendship tae your good self Andy, Bob and Badger. Cheers aye, Gray.

The first ever album/cassette I ever bought was by the Police, including 'Walking on the Moon', 'Roxanne', 'Don't Stand So Close'. That was when I was around eight or nine years old, living in Evanton.

I used to have a bedside rug that had an image of a South American Indian chief's head, with a feather headdress. I remember having experienced a nightmare of that Indian Chief levitating outside my bedroom window. Another regular dream that I experienced a lot of, was one where I was falling from a scaffolding tower, in pitch dark. I always managed to wake up prior to hitting the ground! I always woke with a cold sweat following these experiences.

I am pretty sure my first bike in Evanton was either a purple Chopper/red Raleigh Grifter? I remember one day that I was out on my Chopper. I went flying down a big hill near the house and ended up bashed and bruised and bleeding at the bottom. I ended up gashing my right kneecap. Ross Munro's dad somehow ended up driving me through to the doctor's surgery in Alness, in order to get my wound checked out. Much thanks for that deed. I still bear the scar on my knee from that topsy-turvy moment.

My all time favourite TV programmes that I enjoyed watching in my younger years include the following: *Knight Rider*, *The A-Team*, *Chips* (about the Highway Patrol Police Officers on bikes), *Street Hawk*, *T. J. Hooker*, *Grange Hill*, *Tiswas*, *Top of the Pops*, *The Banana Splits*, *Captain Caveman*, *Huckleberry Hound* ("Ole ma darling – Ole ma darlin" LOL), *Terrahawks*, *Airwolf*, *Miami Vice*, *Little House on the Prairie*, etc.

I don't recall what it was that prompted my mum to decide to move away from Evanton, but one day she decided that the three of us were going to have a new start in Alness (some six to seven miles away).

One of my big memories of being a minor was the realisation of how difficult and awkward times could be only having one parent to come home to after school! 'Divorce' was a word I would come to understand when I developed further on in life.

The Move – A New Start

My Granny Hubbard (my mum's mum) lived in Old Evanton Road in Dingwall. My grandad worked at one of the auction rooms in town. My mum had three brothers, John, Rhoderick and Hamish. She also had a sister, Helen. John ran the Esso filling station in Conon-bridge. Rhodie worked at the saw mill (near my granny's house), and Hamish was a self-employed carpet fitter. I can't recall what my Auntie Helen worked as; I do know that she and her husband ran a great bed and breakfast in Drumnadrochit (near Loch Ness). When my mum decided a move was in order for a new start for the three of us, she had no worries with regards to family support and removals. The family truly mucked in to get the three of us all settled in our new home at 101 Firhill, Alness, Ross-shire.

The final move occurred at night-time, so when we arrived at our new home, there wasn't a great deal to see of the area. Once Margaret and I had both agreed on which room we were having, priority was sleep. To me, the move was all a big adventure of discovery, with new friends to be made, new school, and most of all a new start (fresh) for my mum, Margaret and myself, as well as Duke.

My first reaction after waking up in the morning was to have a look out my bedroom window, in order to survey what Firhill looked like during the day. Then it was downstairs for breakfast, prior to deciding what lay ahead for the rest of the day. Duke was not far behind me when I went downstairs. I let Duke out in the back garden so that he could mark his territory (as dogs do). My mum had since woken and come down for her morning cup of coffee. My mum was not shy in telling me that once we were all settled in our new home, school was a priority. I agreed, as education was vital for future life development.

Our new home was situated on a slight downhill slope, fourth up from the bottom, with an alleyway between our house and the next three houses up. We had a big square at the front of the house, where people used for parking their cars. Later on in life, that square was used to play British bulldogs with our new-found friends.

Our neighbours at 100 Firhill were the Dolans, Effie (mum), Michael, Gerard and Jan. Jan was a little bit of a tomboy… LOL. Effie had three other grown-up daughters, Rosemary, who was a WREN in the Royal Navy (respect to your lovely self, Gray x). Then there was Anne and Tricia. All in all, a very close and loving family and great friends. At 102, we had the Watsons, Pat and Mary. Pat, Stuart, Scott and Lisa, another lovely family and friends, who all made us feel truly welcome to the area. On the opposite side to the square lived the McGills, next door to them were the McGroartys – Jim, Ealnor, Harry, Alison and Carol. They had a wee dog called Sally, who was full of character (like most dogs). Next door to them lived the Wilsons, Tracy, Jimmy and Alan, Janette (mum).

During my residence at 101 Firhill, neighbours came and went. Once Mum, Margaret and I and Duke were finally settled and sorted in our new home, it was decided that education was in order. And so Mum took us along to Coulhill Primary School, where I was put into Primary Five, I remember my teacher's name was Mrs Quacker, a lovely teacher, that she was.

I still remember my only ever bad experience with school dinners. Fish fingers were being served one day. I remember sitting down looking forward to indulging in my lunch. When I was cutting my lunch up, I discovered what appeared to be a fish eye. That experience put me off eating fish fingers for a long time.

I don't have much recollection of the year when I was in Primary Five. I do however remember that my mum ended up back in hospital with her depression. Margaret and I ended up with a family friend who lived beside the Perrins Centre, at the top of Alness High Street. The War Memorial was close by. Isobel Ross looked after the Centre; she used to give Margaret and me a packet of crisps, a piece of fruit and 50 pence every morning, prior to us setting off for school.

I will never forget one night that Margaret and I were heading to the swimming pool (which was over the bridge, by Alness Academy). We were level with the outdoor bowling green (at the back of the Perrins Centre). We never reached the bridge as some man hung himself in the middle of the bridge. We went straight back to tell Isobel, and she called the police. A very traumatic incident that nobody should ever have to witness.

After a certain individual from school had established that I was getting crisps, fruit and 50 pence for school every day, that individual then decided to start waiting for my arrival at school each morning, and used bullying tactics to gain my crisps, fruit and money. This went on for some time, and I adapted a fearful thought that had I reported the matter to a teacher, the consequences would have been a lot worse for myself.

By the time the summer holidays had arrived at the end of term in Primary Five, Margaret and I had moved on from the care of Isobel Ross. I speak for myself, and remember that I had been put in a children's home under Social Services.

The home was located right beside Coulhill Primary. I remember one occasion when Dad was on shore leave from the Navy, he travelled up to Alness to take Margaret and me down to Dirleton, East Lothian, for our summer holidays.

Dad always brought us presents/gifts when he came to see Margaret and me. On this occasion he had pencils and coloured pens, as at this stage in my life, I was really into art and drawing/sketching. Dirleton is a village in between North Berwick and Gullane. This is where my Grandad and Granny Culton lived. Other family members were Uncle Eddie and Aunt Muriel. Their sons were Calum, Andrew and Neil. My Aunt Ina was also here. Uncle Eddie worked in the grounds of Dirleton Castle. Aunt Muriel was a busy bee, always doing work for the village as well as a very caring member of the community. Aunt Ina was a widow; she loved her cats.

One of the things that I liked about the location of Dirleton was that it was situated on the east coast, and had an amazing stretch of gold sand. Edinburgh was not far away either. There was always a hive of positive activities for all ages in Dirleton. North Berwick had a brilliant outdoor swimming pool with a massive slide (well it was massive to me every time I went there). One of the other positive attributes to North Berwick was my Uncle Douglas and Auntie Carol. Dougie, as I called him, served in the Merchant Navy – respect to him. I remember my Auntie Carol used to work in a video shop in town; she always gave us a heads-up on new releases.

Back in Dirleton, my granny and grandad had two King Charles spaniels – Toby and Benji. One of them was black and white – Toby – and Benji was light brown and white. Haddington was not far away from Dirleton. Aunt Muriel's mum, Joey, lived here. Joey was lovely (RIP her dear soul). Later on in life, I discovered that Fish from Marillion came from Haddington. AWESOME – Marillion truly are a great band with truly awesome music. GRAY.

My dad has another brother, Jim Culton. He married Viv and they have two children, Claire and Ian. Jim was a Major in the British Army – respect and salute to you, Uncle Jim, Gray.

I hold and treasure many great and fond and positive memories of my childhood. I will always cherish these memories close to my heart until the day I die.

I am not by any means getting morbid. I am just reflecting

on life, and realising that life is/can be too short to live with regret. Robbie Williams' song 'No Regrets' says a lot of what I mean. I truly respect and admire Robbie for so many positive reasons. Many of his songs I have been able to relate to and empathise with. "Robbie," as Rihanna once sang, "Please don't stop the music". Kind and best and positive wishes and respect to you and family. Cheers aye, Gray.

WEDNESDAY 20TH MARCH 2013

I have just heard on Island FM, courtesy of James Bentley (DJ) and Claire Brouard (news reader) that today is International World Happiness Day. Awesome. Island FM is a truly Absolutely – Awesomely – Amazing radio station playing great songs in the Bailiwick of Glorious Guernsey. The station is informative of so many positive upcoming events and daily occurrences. The team consists of the following great individuals: The Gaffer (Boss) Mike Huston, the DJ's James Bentley, Richard Harding, Carl Ward (Carlos), Andy Newman, Andrew Senneck, Joff Hopkins, Marky-T (Trenchard) and the Legend that is Freddie T. These are all the Diamond Geezers of the Show, and then we have the lovely ladies Brandi Dawson DJ (Brandi runs sessions of Zumba), Laura Clayton (News Editor), Claire Brouard (news reader), Sally Chaddock, Amanda Prigent and Nicole De Garis. I once wrote a short poem for all at Island FM. I would like to share that poem with all readers.

Gonnae (going) to get with the STEREO MCS and Get connected tae (to) Island FM.
Where you'll find quite a few DIAMONDS (Geezers), as well as quite a few GEMS (lovely ladies).
To hear the positive sounds (TUNEAGE) that fills the airwaves of the Bailiwick... Always seems to fulfil – Just the Trick.
Get that 'Good Feeling' with Flo Rida
Find Yourself in 'Paradise' with Coldplay
Surround yourself with 'Happiness' with Goldfrapp
Scream-shout 'Read All About it' with Emeli Sande
'Relax-take it easy' with Mika.

To everyone at Island FM, thank you for all the great and positive service that you All provide. Truly and forever appreciated. Gray (AKA – The Bear).

I truly value and appreciate your friendship, support and continued encouragement and inspiration and motivation. Gray.

Getting back to the book… To some, you may find my method of writing confusing, strange, whatever! I am endeavouring to give as many people that I can, an insight into what it is like walking in my shoes, as well as the view from my eyes, living on a day-to-day basis with the following symptoms:

1) Complex post-traumatic stress disorder (PTSD)
2) Autism
3) Obsessive compulsive disorder (OCD)
4) Attention Deficit hypersensitivity disorder (ADHD)
5) Personality disorder (Border)
6) Recurrent depression
7) Nervous disposition
8) Tinnitus – hearing impairment

Other positive memories that I had from childhood whilst on school holidays include the following:

1) I remember an occasion being taken to the Aviation Museum, which was always full of great sights and (strangely) smells! The one attraction that sticks out in my mind was the Avro Vulcan Bomber which saw many sorties during the Falklands Campaign. I have been fortunate enough in my lifetime to have witnessed a Vulcan Bomber in flight at one of the many airshows that I have attended in the past (Bournemouth).

2) North Berwick was renowned for holding summer Harbour Carnivals. One carnival I remember attending was honoured by the presence of the Pipes and Drums from The Royal Scots Dragoon Guards. Much respect and admiration to both the Regiment and the Band. Cheers aye, Gray.

3) Dirleton was renowned for holding village/church fêtes. My Aunts Muriel and Ina were always involved with these. I remember one particular fête, of which had a VIP guest! There was a new film out at that time, and the story was about a Young Sherlock Holmes with Robert Downey Jnr.

4) With Dirleton being located on the east coast of the Firth of Forth, it had a great stretch of beach with golden sands. Many great memorable times were spent there with Dad, Margaret, cousins Neil, Gary and Lynn, and myself. (Gary and Lynn were my dad's sister Patricia's children; they were living in Prestonpans).

I remember having been to the beach one day with them, and I ended up with bad sunburn to the back of my legs, so much so that my legs ended up blistered! That was a valuable lesson learned – to take more care in the future whilst enjoying the glorious sunshine weather. Cheers aye, Gray.

I have one recollection of a fond memory whilst on holiday in Dirleton. A family get-together had been arranged at my granny's house, Uncle Dougie, Aunt Carol, Aunts Muriel and Ina were there. I remember hearing Opus, 'Life is Life', as well as The Village People's 'YMCA'. A great time was had by all.

Getting back to life in Alness, time had moved on and after another great summer holiday in Dirleton, a new year with a new teacher in Primary Six in Coulhill Primary, with Mr Haldane teaching new/advanced subjects. Mum at this time was back in hospital, and I found myself back in care with Social Services.

I remember being outside in the courtyard of the children's home one light night. One minute I was speaking to another lad from the home, and the next thing I remember was coming around inside nursing a bleeding nose! Whilst outside before, that other lad took a hyper-spell and ended up punching me in the face, resulting in me falling over and banging my head on the concrete slabbing. (Another case of head trauma.)

I remember my first fight in the playground whilst in P6. I can't remember the whole motive behind the scrap, but what I do remember is that it never solved much, except for getting the two of us in detention. Oh yes! – the fight did result in myself ending up with a nose the shape of a ski-jump… laughing ecstatically!

A valuable life and personal lesson was learned from that fight. That being to learn to control and compose myself, with regards to addressing issues linked/attached to my anger emotion. (It's all about learning to transform underlying anger issues from negative to positive.) Cheers aye, Gray.

A positive outcome/result is far better than a negative one! Too much negativity in life can and will create a lot of negative consequences in the long run, if they are not addressed properly and positively. I am speaking from my own personal experiences, as you will discover and realise later on this book. I am talking about problems regarding relationship breakdowns, social issues, financial issues and most importantly of all – Health Issues – Physically – Mentally – Psychologically – Socially.

Throughout my own life journey/voyage, I have adopted coping strategies of dealing with a vast array/spectrum of issues, predominantly negative ones. Cheers aye, Gray.

As I am currently writing my memoirs, I am listening to the 'Spirit of the Glen – Journey – The Royal Scots Dragoon Guards' CD. Their music to me is truly all of the following – Inspiring, Calming, Motivational, Sensational, Positively Grounding – and I find the music helps to drown out my high pitched white noise tone, caused by tinnitus (constant ringing or buzzing in the ears) – definition from my *Oxford Mini Dictionary and Thesaurus.*

I am now listening to the soldiers' brilliant new album. My same comments and thoughts regarding the RSDGs go to the soldiers' music. Much admirable respect, appreciation and great thanks to Colour Sergeant Richie Maddocks, Lance Corporal Ryan Idzi and Sergeant Major Gary Chilton. My sincere thoughts are with you all as well as your loved ones. Wishing you guys all the very best for your futures. Best and positive regards. Gray. POSITIVE RESPECT and THANKS to 1st The Queen's Dragoon Guards and all of their families and loved ones. Gray.

Once again… summer holidays came round and I can remember being on Princess Street in Edinburgh one day with cousin Neil. We were stood in the queue in the Wimpy waiting to be served, when I spotted one of the Dundee United players (from that time). I mentioned to Neil and he confirmed whom I believed the player to be… Dave Bowman. A tangerine moment for any Dundee United supporter… Eh – Gordon Brookes? (Brooksie). Brooksie was with the Gordon Highlanders – By DAND. I met him amongst other great lads whilst attached to the 1st Battalion Royal Highland Fusiliers (White Maff) (Bosnia UNPROFOR – 94–95). Admirable respect tae awe the lads. Gray.

A positive trigger has just reminded me about a memory of when I was younger! My Granny Culton took Margaret and me to Edinburgh Zoo one day. Granny was setting out the picnic table, and whilst she was doing so, I wandered across to the penguin enclosure. There weren't any birds around at the time, so with my back to the mesh fencing I started bouncing off it like an upright trampoline! Little was I aware that a penguin saw me, came up behind and pecked me on a tender region of my body! Another valuable lesson learned quickly, with regards to not intimidating a bird's habitat or private space/comfort zone. (And before anyone comments… I was talking about the feathered species – bird. LOL. Any Army/Forces banter welcome.)

I remember my last years as a primary school student. My classroom was a large hut down the hill from the main school building. We had the school sports field and sand pit outside. Mrs Holt was the teacher's name. Respect to her. Gray.

During registration in the mornings, Mrs Holt always read out my name in the register as Robert. I prefer Graham Robert Culton. I was born on the 25th January 1975, which is coincidentally Robert Burns Day, Robbie being a famous Scottish poet.

MY LOVE IS LIKE A RED, RED ROSE

O, MY LOVE IS LIKE A RED, RED ROSE,
THAT'S NEWLY SPRUNG IN JUNE.
O, MY LOVE IS LIKE A MELODY,
THAT SWEETLY PLACED IN JUNE.

AS FAIR THOU ART, MY BONNIE LASS.
SO DEEP IN LOVE AM I.
AND I WILL LOVE THEE, STILL MY DEAR,
TILL A'THE SEAS GANG DRY.

TILL A'THE SEAS GANG DRY, MY DEAR
AND THE ROCKS MELT WI' THE SUN!
AND I WILL LOVE THEE, STILL MY DEAR,
WHILE THE SANDS OF LIFE SHALL RUN.

AND FARE THE WEEL, MY ONLY LOVE!
AND FARE THE WELL AWHILE!
AND I WILL COME AGAIN, MY LOVE.
THO IT WERE TEN THOUSAND MILE!

BY ROBERT BURNS

I don't recall the year, although I do remember one night seeing a big orange glow in the direction of Coulhill Primary! Curiosity got the better of me, and I decided to go and investigate the cause of the glow.

As I got to the Community Centre and shops, I realised the glow was caused by part of the school ablaze! The fire brigade and police were already at the scene, endeavouring to both extinguish the flames, as well as trying to prevent the fire from spreading to other parts of the school. Admirable respect to the emergency services and investigation team involved in the aftermath of the act of arson by mindless yobs.

The Education Department, along with other resources, would have had their normal work routine strained during the aftermath of the fire, in trying to sort out alternative classrooms for the school pupils that were affected through damage to their classrooms. It would have been priority for Education to arrange for temporary classrooms, in order that the pupils' education was not affected.

During the weekends, the Firhill posse used to get together and have a laugh and chill out. Bonfire nights were great times. Everyone used to muck in with positive spirits with regards to collecting wood for our bonfire. The biggest challenge we all had was getting a centre-post. Come the nights of 5th November, we all had a bonfire to be proud of, where everyone was welcome to attend. Awesome respect to all involved for great memories. Cheers aye, Gray.

BIG SHOUT to the following friends: Jason Brown (Ninja), John and George Robertson, Derek and Gary Welch, Jo and Brian Foy, James McCabe, Jimmy Wilson, Steven Shaw, Paddy Daw, Pat, Stewart and Scott Watson, Carol McGroarty, Sharon Daw, Tracy Wilson, Jan Dolan, my sister Mags (sorry about the Dripper! – Gray), Barry and John Martin. RESPECT to you awe. Cheers aye, Gray.

ALNESS ACADEMY YEARS

Alness Academy was located at the north end of Alness, near the A9, running up to Wick and John O'Groats. The logo for the Academy badge was of an oystercatcher (a bird), the main logo was black with a green background. The reason behind the oystercatcher was simply because there were always oystercatchers nesting on the Academy roof. With the Academy being located so near to the Cromarty Firth, it was an obvious habitual nesting area.

Stepping up from primary to secondary education created a mixture of feelings for me – deep within! More advanced learning (subjects), new teachers (tutors) as well as making new friends from different family backgrounds to mine. Apprehensive feelings would be the most appropriate term to describe my feelings.

Registration on the first day at the Academy took a little longer for obvious reasons, discovering all about our weekly timetable, also finding out our new tutor names for all the new subjects that were waiting for us all to be educated in (undertaken). Like my name for registration whilst in Primary Seven , 'Robert' was the name used by all of my tutors.

The new subjects that I was to undertake during my years at the Academy included the following: O grade English, Geography, History, Physical Education (P.E.), Standard Grade Maths, Science, as well as Music, Art, Computing, Religious Education (R.E.) and French and Home Economics and Woodwork.

The first week in Year One at the Academy took some getting used to, what with finding my way around the complex corridors from one subject area to the next, as well as getting to know new subject tutors names! Considering what Margaret and I saw the night we were due to go swimming (whilst we were in the care of Isobel at the Perrins Centre), walking to the Academy Monday to Friday, had no psychological affect on myself, every time I walked over the railway bridge!

Week two of Year One at the Academy was obviously easier than that of week one, as I was gradually getting into a routine, with guidance from my trusty timetable.

If somebody was to ask me now to remember a happy memory of my years at the Academy? One fond memory that comes to mind is one where I found myself in detention (for misbehaviour!). Tutors took it in turn to oversee detentions. I remember (one of my many detentions) and Mr Meikle (Robert), the Academy Rector, was in the hot seat! Mr Meikle was an Armed Forces veteran – much admirable respect to your good self sir. Cheers aye, Gray.

Mr Meikle would spend time talking of truly inspirational stories of his service to HM Queen and Country. His stories were truly awesome in my eyes.

My favourite subjects were as follows: English, Geography, Science, Computing, P.E., Woodwork and French. I did enjoy my other subjects, so no offence to my tutors of the subjects not listed as favourites. Cheers aye, Gray.

Life at home was OK. Mum was on medication for her depression. Mum was Mum! She was always looking for practical things to do, in order to keep her mind occupied and herself motivated. Mum enjoyed cooking and baking. I'm sure she got these traits from my Granny Hubbard. Every time I stayed at my Granny's, she always had a lovely home-baked coffee sponge with a coffee butter cream filling in the middle, safely tucked inside a cake tin in her food larder.

I remember one time, where my mum decided to get me a pet, seeing as Margaret had Duke. I ended up with a black cat called Sooty. After a while, Margaret and I came to a mutual agreement whereas I would have Duke and she would have the cat. An agreement that we both realised that Margaret was more a cat person, as I was a dog person!

When the weekends arrived, I would take Duke for long walks up to the woods or down by the Averon River. We both loved to get out for those walks. I never let Duke off the lead as he had a tendency to run off, and the time he had the opportunity, he would be gone for ages!

I remember a couple of occasions at the Academy, when during Home Economics lessons, the tutor told the boys that we were going to make boxer shorts! I can't remember what the girls would be making! We had to provide our own cloth material. I told Mum later that day, and within a couple of days, she got me some material with Jelly Babies (as a design). Bless Mum, she had great taste. I was the only student to end up with Jelly Baby boxer shorts.

I enjoyed Science lessons for many reasons! I had some great friends, including the following: Andrew Hossack (Andy), Craig Hebson, Gary MacLeod.

We always endeavoured to enjoy the lessons that we were taught by our tutor Mrs Dunn. I was renowned at times for getting myself red carded for minor disruptive behaviour! LOL. I'm pretty sure Andy and Craig would have a few good memories from our days in the Science lab! When I got myself red carded, I always found myself in the store room at the back of the lab. LOL. I thoroughly enjoyed English and Geography classes. I found them very educational and informative.

I had the hots for a girl in Geography, her name was Sharon Connelly. I remember one night having a secret meet-up with Sharon, up by Obsdale Primary School. Another happy memory from my time at secondary school. Sharon and I are friends on Facebook. I am glad to hear that she got married and now has her own family. Kind and best wishes to you and your family, Sharon. Cheers aye, Gray.

I vaguely remember my first Academy dance! I do remember Status Quo and their track 'In the Army' was played during the dance. Mum ended up back in hospital during my three years at the Academy. I remember on one occasion that she went back in (following an attempt at taking her own life) I ended up staying with my granny at her house in Old Evanton Road in Dingwall. In order that my education was not affected at Alness Academy, I was given a bus pass, so that I could get the bus through to Alness. Highland

Omnibuses was the bus operator. The reason I was able to continue attending Alness Academy was due to the fact that I was settled with a familiar routine. It would not have been beneficial for me to start going to Dingwall Academy.

I remember on one occasion, whilst during an English lesson, someone discovered some matches in the room. I ended up striking one of them (whilst the tutor had his back turned). I'm pretty sure the tutor was called Mr Mather – respect to his good self, he was a brilliant tutor. Cheers aye, Gray. Following my act of stupidity, and once the smell of burnt match had made itself known in the room, Mr Mathers challenged as to whom was responsible. Silence fell on the situation! And so Mr Mathers stated that if the culprit was not prepared to accept responsibility, then he would put everyone in detention. At this I stood up and admitted that I was responsible. Then the bell went, and Mr Mathers dismissed the rest of the class for break. I, however, sat through break in detention as punishment for my act of stupidity. Ah well, some of the class had a laugh at the expense of my stupid/foolish act.

My Uncles Hamish and Rhoderick went up to Inverness regularly to visit Mum in hospital. When they did I would go up with them to help lift Mum's spirits. Mum truly loved and enjoyed her visits, just as much as I enjoyed seeing her. The only time I hated the visits, was when it came time to say goodbye!

The sport that I truly enjoyed during P.E. lessons was swimming. Mike Stainke was my tutor, and an awesome one at that. Cheers aye, Gray. I remember that the Academy basketball team were playing one of their matches in Blairgowrie (I think). A trip and coach was organised for the students to go down and show their support. It was a truly great day for all that attended. Much admirable respect to Andrew Torrie and Andrew Menzies and Colin Proctor and Gary Smith and the rest of the basketball team. Cheers aye, Gray.

The first time I ever went abroad was through a ski holiday whilst at the academy. The resort was Serre Chevalier in France. I was too excited about the trip the night before we were picked up by coach at the Academy. I ended up doing an all-nighter (staying awake). I had Peter Waterman and Michaela Strachan to watch in the programme *The Hitman and Her.*

When the time came to leave the house in the morning, I said cheerio to Mum and Duke, Margaret was still asleep, and I trundled down to the Academy with my luggage. When I met up with friends by the coach, I could sense the awesome hype of excitement, everyone was buzzing with ecstatic excitement.

Gill Sharpe (Mrs) was the tutor responsible for checking that we were all present on the coach prior to departing for Dingwall and Fort Augustus Academy, both students and tutors. Once everyone was accounted for, the coaches rolled out of Fort Augustus Academy grounds, setting out in convoy formation for Glasgow Airport.

Our flight from Glasgow was to Lyon Airport, and then a coach trip to the Serre Chevalier Resort. It was night-time by the time we arrived at the hotel. My cousin Hamish was on the same trip. Hamish went to either Dingwall/ Fort Augustus Academy. Being as this was my first time experiencing skiing, I was in the beginners group. I have one recollection of the trip: we had been on one of the runs in the morning and it had been decided to meet up for lunch. One of the skills that we had been taught was the 'Snow Plough Stop'. I was skiing towards the rendez-vous point on a gentle slope. I saw the restaurant/lodge, which had a lot of other holidaymakers dotted about, most of whom were chatting. I endeavoured to apply the snow-plough principles. Unfortunately my skills were not up to scratch… resulting in myself skiing into a French holidaymaker, coming to a halt, and at the same time the gentleman ended up with a broken ski pole! Luckily, after I made my apologies, Mrs Sharp was at hand to sort out the matter in a positive manner. My sincere apologies to that gentleman and much thanks and respect to Gill Sharp for being my Saviour. Cheers aye, Gray.

BOOZE was a no-go area for all students. However, I remember one night, the temptation of alcohol got the better of a couple of individuals! Mrs Sharp was once again at hand to deal with the individuals. I remember hearing Mrs Sharp asking one of the students, "Have you been drinking?" The response that followed was somewhat humorous for others. The answer was the following, "Yes. Mrs… I have had a couple of pizzas." LOL.

All in all, the skiing trip was a great holiday had by all, a holiday that I hold many memorable and positive experiences.

During my second year at the Academy, I once again fell victim to the hands of psychological abuse from a certain individual bully. I experienced both physical and verbal abuse from that person, and each time I lived in fear of repercussions had I reported him to a tutor.

I don't recall much of my third and final year at Alness Academy. However, I will always remember all of the brilliant tutors that taught in a positive and professional manner. Truly and forever appreciated. I will also remember all the many and awesome friends that I made. I truly appreciate and value your friendship – NOW – FOREVER – ALWAYS. Cheers aye, Gray.

COLLEGE AND TA SERVICE

During my last term at Alness Academy, whilst using the library for study purposes, I became aware of a Bakers Course at Inverness Technical College. Following that positive moment of discovery, I decided to get the ball rolling with regards to getting enrolled on the course. One of the first steps I had to take was to contact the Education Department in Dingwall, with regards the course, and at the same time applying for a bursary, in order that I could get the funding to purchase my baker's whites and appropriate tools for the course.

By this time, Mum was back at home and getting on in life as best that she could (even though she was on a lot of medication).

My first day at college was a little like my first day at the Academy... slightly apprehensive to start with, that apprehension soon evaporated as my time at college on the course progressed. If I remember rightly, my tutor was a gentleman called Dave Skeoch. He certainly knew his stuff. Some of the new fellow students that I befriended were: Graham Powell from Gairloch-Wester Ross, his niece Sandra also fae Gairloch. Two lovely lassies fae the Fort William area, Alyson Bryson and Dawn Rankin. There was a lad called Paul fae Elgin, as well as a lad called Keny fae Nairn. There was another lovely lass called Rhonda who if I remember rightly was fae Inverness. There was a lad by the name of George, I'm pretty sure he was from Forres. My apologies to anyone else that was on the course. My mind is not as young now as it was back then. Gray.

Life at the college was brilliant. It had a common room (Com) where students could go during tea breaks and lunch. They also had a cafeteria. Students had the choice of using the café at lunch or the other option was to drift into town for the wide selection of food establishments. It was all personal preference!

What I enjoyed most about the Com was the fact that it had a jukebox and pool tables. There was always a great selection of songs to be played and heard by all. It was also a great place to socialise with others.

I was 15 years old when I left Alness Academy to attend Inverness Technical College of Further Education.

At one point during my term on the course, there was a competition run by Hovis. All students were eligible to enter. I was very surprised when the results were announced following the competition! I was awarded 1st prize for my Hovis granary loaves, and also received a commendation for my Hovis bloomers. I was well pleased with my efforts and achievements.

It came to my attention at one point that a band by the name of Runrig was having a concert at Inverness ice rink. I had heard a lot of positive things about Runrig. Dawn Rankin's birthday was the same day as the concert, and so I bought her a birthday card, and on the night of the concert, I went to the ice rink in the hope of catching up with Donnie Munro, Calum and Rory Macdonald, Peter Wishart, Malcolm Jones and Iain Bayne (the band members of Runrig).

My patience and hanging around – awaiting the arrival of the lads – paid off positively. I managed to get all of Runrig to sign Dawn's birthday card, and wished them all a great performance. I then made tracks into town where I believed Dawn was out celebrating with friends. She was truly delighted with her birthday card, and even more overwhelmed to discover that Runrig had signed it.

I was informed one day at college by Graham Powell, that he knew of a place in Inverewe (near Gariloch) that they were looking for a baker for the summer season. The employer was the National Trust for Scotland. Inverewe has Trust land – namely Inverewe Gardens – situated by Loch Ewe. Thanks to Graham enlightening me about the job, I went ahead and applied for the position. I got the number to phone, and spoke to a lovely lady by the name of Moira Crook. Coincidentally, I was offered an interview the following day, and Graham was driving back to Gairloch and offered me a lift to Inverewe in order that I could attend the interview.

I stayed at an old hostel (owned by Inverewe Gardens), then took a walk up to the 'Big House' the next morning for the interview with Moira and Professor Henderson (who was in charge of the gardens and management). The interview went really well and I was successful in landing the job, with accommodation included at the hostel.

Having a self-reflective moment on that very memorable and positive experience of getting my first taste of independence away from home, is truly overwhelming. Much thanks and admiration to Moira and Professor Henderson for giving me that great opportunity. Truly and forever appreciated. Cheers aye, Gray.

Following my interview, I caught the Royal Mail post bus to Achnasheen train station, from where I was to catch the train back to Inverness, in order that I could get back home to share my great news with Mum.

(Achnasheen was a somewhat remote area of Wester Ross. There is a scene from the movie *Trainspotting* where the lads jump on a train and end up in a very remote part of Scotland! That is how I relate Achnasheen to.)

Saturday 13th April 2013. I am currently sitting in my 'Safe Haven' at the Manor – Room 104. Whilst writing I am listening to Island FM's Breakfast Show. Today there is a father/son duo presenting – Richard and Jon Harding.

Much respect, thanks and admiration to you both. Cheers aye, Gray. Listening to Rod Stewart's 'Baby Jane'. Both an awesome singer/songwriter – song – played by an awesome DJ duo. I have got Rod's album, 'Some Guys Have All the Luck', in my wide/varied CD collection. Absolutely – Awesomely – Amazing. Cheers Rod. Gray.

Richard played 'Love Hurts' by the awesome band Blue earlier! Coincidentally, blue is my favourite colour, and my bestest mate (Bro) is nicknamed 'Blue' (Karl Noble). Miss Ya Bro, Gray. I remember when the band Blue had an entry in the last Eurovision Song Contest. I got somewhat tearful/emotional whilst listening to 'Love Hurts' earlier! James Bentley from Island FM once said during a previous morning show that "Certain songs performed by certain musicians can create a trigger"! What do I mean by the term trigger? I am not referring to the component that you would associate with a weapon, I am however referring to a song that triggers an individual's memory to a past life event! That trigger can create a reflective moment of remembrance in one of two ways. These being either 'positive' or 'negative'. My perspective of life has been two-fold! At times it has been a journey, others a voyage. This will become more apparent throughout *See Me For Who I Am*. Cheers aye, Gray.

When I got back to the hostel in Inverewe, I met a lady by the name of Jean, whom was employed as the warden. I got the key to my room and unpacked my clothes and stuff, before taking a walk up to Poolewe village. There was two hotels, a village shop/post office, craft shop, doctor's surgery and a pub/restaurant with a pool table and jukebox in the village.

The next day, I woke up early as I was very keen to get started in my new job as the baker at Inverewe Gardens Restaurant. I was greeted at the restaurant by Moira and Pearl McIver. Pearl was the chef/cook. No sooner was I at my work area, the sound of the large Hobart mixer was in full motion mixing the bread dough to be used to make fresh rolls.

I had a wide variety of bakery goods to bake and make prior

to the restaurant opening for the season (summer) to the public. Products including the following: bread rolls, scones, pancakes, meringues, shortbread (including caramel), sweet pastry for cherry, ginger, farmhouse, fruit slices (similar range to Mr Kipling), chocolate crispie slice, apple pie, Danish pastry, puff pastry for pearl. I was responsible for doing the ordering of ingredients for my products as and when required.

Social life away from work was good. From time to time there would be a band organised to play at the village hall, and on one occasion, an amazingly awesome band – Wolfstone – were hired to come and play a gig. The band truly rocked the night away. Coincidentally, Wolfstone members come from the Ardross area near Alness.

We had a lovely team at the restaurant, including the following lovely ladies – Theresa and Ellen, Penny Crook, Donna Baker, Sandra (Supervisor), Alison. (Having difficulty remembering the names of other lovely members of the team!) No disrespect. Agnes was another one I remember. Wendy fae Edinburgh was another.

Due to my arrival at Inverewe, and the lack of knowledge of myself, I was not challenged straight away with regards being served in the village pubs. I believe my height gave the impression to bar staff that I was old enough to purchase/consume alcohol! Well! This was to be short-lived! After a couple of weeks, word got around the area that the new baker at Inverewe Restaurant was only 15. Ah well – onwards and upwards.

During my day off each week, I tended to catch the Wester Bus with Ali the driver – through to Inverness to spend my wages, sometimes I would go home and see Mum and Duke, others I would go and visit my Granny Hubbard.

On one particular trip to Inverness, I discovered that Runrig were having the release of a new album, namely 'The Big Wheel'. I was over the moon at having an excellent opportunity to buy their new album, get it signed by Donnie Munro, Peter Wishart, Calum and Rory Macdonald, Malcolm Jones and Iain Bayne. By the time I walked round to Woolworths (in the High Street) there was a good-sized queue of people excitedly awaiting to get their albums signed by the band. So I duly took my place in the queue and awaited my awesome chance to meet the guys. When my turn came around, my legs were like jelly due to having an amazing opportunity of meeting my (to be) lifelong music heroes.

It wasn't just ladies in the restaurant team, there was a guy called John Holland (who was a former Queen's Own Highlander). Then there was another by the name of Kelso. If I remember correctly, John was fae Dunfermline Fife, and Kelson fae Edinburgh.

There were some mad parties held at the hostel, following pub closing time. Never to the extent that the hostel got trashed. I remember on one occasion, John and Kelson acquired a putt-putt scooter! They were like little kids on Christmas day with it – LOL. Their excitement rubbed off on me somewhat! They both decided to allow me a turn on their new toy, I in turn took a spin up to the garden's coach and car park. The best part was coming back down the hill to the hostel.

My first summer season working at the restaurant came to an abrupt end one night, a night I was feeling a little hyper and mischievous! I went down to the far end of the hostel – John's room was there. I went outside to John's window (he was sleeping), I decided to knock on his window and wake him up.

John eventually woke up and was in the process of saying to me, "Graham! Stop knocking on the window afore you..." at that moment I finished his sentence for him. My left hand penetrated the glass pane, resulting in a bad laceration to my wrist! At this point John was wide awake, and was rushing out to me in order to administer first aid. His military first aid training skills were still fresh within him.

By now I had gone into a state of shock, enhanced by the amount of blood emitting from my wound.

I was wearing Joe Bloggs dungarees, with a Hearts away top, as well as a pair of white British Knights demi sports trainers at the time of the accident. The boots and my dungarees turned red immediately. By this time, Theresa had heard the commotion, and came out of her room to investigate and assist. She told me to get into the kitchen, which I did; in turn, she ran the cold water tap. I went to put my wrist to the running water. Theresa screamed at me not to do so, prior to her wetting a teal towel and applying to my wound. During these proceedings, John had gone to Moira's house to inform her of what had occurred. Moira took the car down to collect me and take me to the doctor's surgery in Poolewe.

The doctor dressed my wound and called for an ambulance. Due to the remote location of Poolewe on the west coast, the ambulance either came from Dingwall or Inverness. Whilst awaiting the paramedics' arrival, Moira sat with me giving me constant reassurance, whilst keeping my spirits up with humour. I truly appreciate and am forever thankful to Moira, John, Theresa, the doctor and the paramedics that came to take me to Raigmore Hospital in Inverness in order to have my wrist operated on and patched up. Cheers aye, Gray.

I ended up going to theatre in the early hours, and when I woke up, I was surprised to see my sister Margaret. Moira must have phoned my mum after I left Poolewe in the ambulance to inform her what had occurred.

When I was given my discharge paper, Margaret informed me that Mum was at Granny's, so we caught the bus to Conon Bridge, where both Mum and Granny were relieved to see me. I never had the time to get a clean change of clothes following the accident, and so had to make do with my blood-stained Joe Bloggs dungarees, until I returned to Inverewe later on. I must have looked a right sight to others! Later on that day, I caught a bus through to Dingwall in order to catch the bus back up to Inverewe. Ali was somewhat shocked to see me when he pulled up at the bus stop in the Wester Bus!

On my return back to the hostel, I was greeted with a hug

from Theresa and Ellen, then John came through to see how I was doing. The next morning up at the restaurant, I was greeted by another two hugs, one from Moira, the other from Pearl. Both ladies were mums, and their hugs were very compassionate. The three of us sat in the staff room with a coffee, prior to the rest of the team rocking in – ready to start work.

A plan of action was agreed between Moira, Pearl and myself with regards to getting someone from the team to shadow me for a couple of days in order that I could train them up in mixing methods for the range of bakery products. Once this was achieved, it was decided best for myself to finish my contract, and go back home to allow my wrist to heal.

Mum was relieved to see me when I walked in the front door, probably just as much as Duke was glad to see me. I was still able to take Duke out for long walks (on the lead!). He had a high tendency to run off for hours on end whenever the opportunity arose for him (which, on a good few occasions, he took advantage of).

Prior to saying my goodbyes to the team at Inverewe, I was given assurance that I would be welcome to return to the restaurant the following summer season.

When my wrist had had time to heal, I was able to go back to college to finish off my course, prior to leaving first time round, following my securing the job in Inverewe.

One of my many fond memories during two seasons working

at Inverewe Gardens Restaurant, was the morning I met Ulrika Johnson. GMTV had sent Ulrika out on a road trip around the UK. Ulrika was doing a roaming weather report from different locations up and down the country. One of those locations just happened to be Inverewe Gardens. I don't think Ulrika was too impressed with the wet west coast weather, neither was she impressed by the local population of Scottish midgies.

I never got to meet the lovely lady, although I was able to acquire a signed GMTV postcard of her lovely self. Cheers aye, Gray. Another lovely lady that I had a missed opportunity of meeting whilst working at Inverewe was Pam St Clement – Pat Butcher from *Eastenders.* As soon as I found out Pat had just been in the restaurant I nipped up to the visitor centre/ car park to see if I could meet her. Pat must have gone for a look around the gardens.

One of my specialities at the restaurant was Danish pastries. I always had two very excited tasters waiting patiently for me to remove the first batch from the multi-deck oven. The aroma of freshly baked Danish enhanced the kitchen/bakery area for sometime after. Moira and Pearl were always nearby as soon as they sensed the Danish aroma.

During the season, the gardens had regular coach visits. I remember WALLACE ARNOLD were one of the main coach operators bringing hundreds of tourists to the attractive gardens and views around Loch Ewe. The drivers always had some amazing stories to share. I was always guaranteed a great laugh with them. Cheers aye, Gray.

During my second season working at the restaurant, it was

great to see all the friendly faces (from my first time/season) plus there were some new faces/friends to be befriended.

There was a new owner of the Poolewe Hotel. His name, if I remember right, was Johanas, who was almost a giant! Johanas was from Iceland, he played for Celtic during his life journey. Respect tae the Big Man. Cheers aye, Gray.

Life is a voyage of discovery for us all as individuals. It is by no means always straightforward plain sailing, and we can often be faced with stormy seas (challenges/obstacles) that can have a tendency to let our 'mind bearings' (sense of judgement) to slip and alter course!

It is how we as individuals of the human race tackle/deal with these obstacles/challenges that make us the individuals that we all are. Life would be somewhat monotonous (boring) were it all to be smooth/plain sailing!

Life is for living in a Positive – Harmonic – Peaceful manner. We don't get any second chances at it.

I have been held back in life for way too long now by negative anchors! I am gradually dropping these anchors one by one (slowly and very positively surely)... Thus enabling myself to continue my own personal voyage/journey on a more positive and stress-free course. Cheers aye, Gray.

I have a very 'avid imagination' through my health conditions.

Negative emotions can be so empowering – especially when

you are both physically and mentally exhausted, as well as deprived of regular sleep. Concentration and judgement (eecision making) can truly go to pot/pear-shaped!

LIFE is for living in a safe (positive) environment! We are not given life to abuse/exploit/hate/discriminate other members of the human race! Yet many individuals seem to find it appropriate behaviour to do so!

"Courage is letting go of the familiar to make a brighter future. At times you must walk away from the familiar – to fight for a brighter future." (Anon)

There was also new ownership of the Corriness. Eric's wife was from Canada. During my second season at Inverewe, I found myself attracted to a few ladies. Nicola was one of them; she worked at the Poolhouse Hotel. Nicola was from Australia. Another lassie with whom I shared a short-term relationship with was called Sarah Stewart. Sarah was from Kinlochewe; her dad owned the store there.

During the second season, Wolfstone held another gig in the area, which was attended by many. Sarah and myself included. I even got myself a part-time job working in the 'Chippy Hut' at the garage in Inverewe. The garage was run by a great guy by the name of Jimmy. His lovely wife ran the Chippy Hut. If I remember rightly... her name was Maira?

There was a fatal incident that occurred between the hostel and Poolhouse Hotel one night. An incident that would have life-changing effects on many. RIP Louis. I found it hard trying to get to sleep that night as the flashing blue lights of the police were shining into my room. It was that incident that has lead me to have a big hate for drink drivers!

Sadly, my season at the restaurant was short-lived. I disagreed with one member of staff with regards to him getting a book to record his work hours, and I was not entitled to a book for the hours I worked. In turn, I gave my notice to Moira. I was fortunate to land a job in a bakery in Gairloch, at the local convenience store. I even landed accommodation with the lovely family that ran/owned the store.

I was a serving member of the Territorial Army at this stage in life. My unit was the 2nd Battalion – 51st Highland Volunteers – Queen's Own Highlanders. I was part of the Mortar Platoon at Ferry Road in Dingwall. My first Colour Sergeant was called Aidan Brennan. Much respect and admiration to you (Colour) – Aidan. I truly appreciated your positive advice and words of wisdom. Cheers aye, Gray. The awesome Mortar Platoon consisted of the following Great guys: Eddie M – Peter Legge – Davie B – Big Chris – (Killer) Andy M – Clem – Rab C – Adam – Craig. My second PSI at Dingwall was another great guy – Maurice Stirling. Thanks to yourself Maurice for your positive advice and words of wisdom. Forever appreciated. CFGB. The Boss Man of the Platoon was called Lt Munro.

I was privileged during my time with the Mortars to experience a live shoot down in Salisbury. I was a No 2 on my mortar. My job entailed being married to the 81mm Barrel (figure of speech). My role, once the system was set up, was to (when the order was given) pull the pin from the round and put down the barrel – job done.

The vehicles that we had to enhance our role were one tonne Land Rovers – one tonnies for short.

I hold many great and awesome memories of my time as a member of 2 51 Highland, especially the exercises we were involved with. I remember my first ever flight in a Gazelle helicopter, and also my first flight ever in a Chinook (Woca-wocas as I used to call them!).

We used to have regular range days down by Fort George (on the Moray Firth). I remember one such range day – where we had an officer from Australia over on an exchange programme. I had the opportunity to get my hands on the SLR – Self Loading Rifle (7.62). That rifle packed a right positive punch, hence why someone gave it the title – The Elephant Gun!

The SLR was an effective personal weapon for combat; sadly for many it was to be phased out to a museum piece. To be replaced by the SA-80 (5.56). I have also had many opportunities to fire and get hands on the GPMG (7.62) General Purpose Machine Gun. That system rocks. During one of my many weekends spent at the TA Centre in Elgin, I had the opportunity to get my hands on a Milan post. Of course it wasn't fitted with a live missile as it was a Milan Simulator. I did my TA Recruits Course at Milton Bridge near Penicuick – Edinburgh. The accommodation was wooden Nissan huts. During my service with the TA I completed a two-week camp down at Barry Budden (Barry – Butlins) near Broughty Ferry, Tayside.

When I had worked my notice at Inverewe Restaurant, I was getting myself into a new routine at the bakery in Gairloch, when during one shift I had an unexpected visit from my PSI – Maurice Stirling and the Boss, Lt Murno. It was great seeing them; at first I actually thought they came round to see if they could blag some fresh bread for the troops! It turned out that the Mortars were in Gairloch for the weekend acting as marshals for some Great Western Challenge that was occurring. They both enquired as to how I was enjoying my new job. In honest response, I informed them that I wasn't happy being a baker anymore. I was then invited to join the rest of the Platoon's activities over the weekend, of which I gladly did without hesitation. A massive cheers aye to Maurice, the Boss and all the lLads for an awesome weekend. Forever appreciated. Gray.

Back home in Alness, Mum was out of hospital getting on with life as best she could. Duke was over the moon at me being home, as I was able to take him out for long walks again. No sooner was I settled back into home life, when I decided to go back to college, 'til I came of age to join the British Army. At first I was looking at joining one of the Royal Artillery Regiments. My preference would have been to join the Highland Gunners.

I remember getting home from college one night (got into the house just as the six o'clock news on BBC1 came on). The breaking news story was focused on a 'blue on blue' (friendly fire incident) in Iraq. Eight British troops that were travelling in a Warrior had been shot at by an American A-10 (Tank Buster) plane. I stood in the middle of the living room in disbelief and shocked at the tragic news. As I was to find out at a later date, three of the eight service personnel were from the 1st Battalion Queens Own Highlanders. We will remember them all, CFGB.

ENLISTMENT INTO 1ST BATTALION QUEEN'S OWN HIGHLANDERS

During my lunch break (the next day at college), I went into Inverness town centre, and (figure of speech) marched into the Armed Forces Careers Office, just up from the River Ness. There was a Matlo sat at the front desk; he greeted me with "Good afternoon, how can I help you?" My answer was, "Good afternoon, I'm here to join the Army." Prior to the Matlo going to inform the Army Careers Officer, he endeavoured to persuade me to choose a career in the Royal Navy! Admirable respect and admiration to both the services, as well as his efforts to change my mind with regards to my prior request. My mind was already set in concrete (figure of speech) that I was all ready to offer my service to HM Queen and Country (ARMY).

Five minutes later, I was sat behind a desk with a member of the Army Recruiting Team. The Sergeant gave me some insight into the wide options available in the British Army. He asked me if I was thinking about a career in either Infantry or a Corps. My answer to him was simple and to the point. "1st Battalion Queen's Own Highlanders, Caber Feigh Gu Braith."

At that point, the Sergeant could see by the look in my eyes that my mind was set on me becoming an infantry soldier with one of the finest regiments in the British Army.

Once the Sergeant had completed all the relevant paperwork,

he informed me what would happen during the next couple of weeks, including getting a date to come in and sit my 'Barb Test'. He gave me some paperwork to take away, and get signed by my mum, and he informed me to get that back into the office as soon as I could.

I will never forget the great and positive feelings that I had and felt about myself following what I was setting out to achieve in my life. Becoming a member of a massive organisation, namely the British Army and the 1st Battalion Queen's Own Highlanders.

I was buzzing with excitement by the time I got back to college. Mr Skeoch asked me why I was looking so bright and cheery. So I told him where I had been and also was setting out to do with my life. He responded by saying, "Well done… from baker to soldier."

Travelling back to Alness after college, I was concerned about how Mum was going to take my news about enlisting. By the time I reached the front door of the house, I decided not to tell her straight away, what I would do though would be to ask how she was doing and how her day had been. When I had established that she was in good form and that her day had been a good one, I then decided to share my news with her – that I was going to join the Army.

Before Mum had time to express how she felt about my news, I put the kettle on to make us both a coffee All I was able to do from there on in was to constantly give Mum regular reassurance that I would be okay.

I could tell by the look of apprehension and fear of the unknown look from Mum's eyes that it was going to take an extreme amount of reassurance. At first she was reluctant to sign the parental authorisation sections of my paperwork. I told Mum in a calm and collective tone/mannerism that I wanted to do something positive with my life, as well as gaining some travel and adventure at the same time.

I can't recall how my dad took my news of joining the Army, rather than opting for the Navy and following a career at sea like himself. I used to feel that he was a little disappointed in my chosen service. At the same time, I did manage to pick up a sense of elation that he would support and respect my decision. From childhood to the day I die, my dad has always been, and will forever remain my true hero. MIKE AND THE MECHANICS – 'THE LIVING YEARS', My chosen song of 'Eternal Dedication' to my dad, Raymond Douglas Culton – 'Rocky'.

During the following couple of weeks, my date to sit my 'Barb Test' (entrance exam) for entry into the forces came; on completion of the exam I never had long to wait for my score and options available. The Recruitment Officer came through to the front with a print out of my score. He informed me that I would make a great infantry soldier with the Queen's Own Highlanders. I was truly elated at this point, however I had to compose myself as I still had basic training to pass successfully prior to passing out and joining the 'Blue Maff' (nickname for the Queen's Own Highlanders). CFGB.

The Sergeant then informed me that I would get a date in the post, to come back to the Careers Office and pledge my oath of allegiance. I would also be asked to sign for the 'Queen's Shilling', a long-running Armed Forces tradition, where someone joining either of the three Armed Forces Services is given 15 pounds in order to buy boot polish/ brushes prior to commencing training. My money was used to purchase three pints of Tennent's lager at the bar at the train station. LOL.

Without being disrespectful to the tradition, those pints went down a treat with dignity and respect and three toasts to my future career as an infantry soldier with the 'Blue Maff'.

During the next night of training with the Mortars in Dingwall, I had great pleasure in informing Maurice and the lads that in due course I would be leaving the Platoon to undertake my training to become a qualified infantry soldier amongst the many fine ranks/companies of the 1st Battalion QOH. Coincidentally, once training was finished, the Platoon convened in the bar area and an announcement was made by Adam Gunn that there was going to be a leaving do for two members of the Platoon! These two members were Neil and myself. Following this announcement, the sound of beer cans being opened ensued followed by "best wishes" to both Neil and myself. Another awesome member of the Platoon that I forgot to mention before is Peter Legge fae Invergordon. Sorry to Peter, also Eddie McKenzie – Gary McFarlane and Geordie (Tudor). Cheers aye, lads. Kind and best regards. Gray.

It was disclosed that the leaving bash would be in the form of a Hawaiian night. Bermuda shorts, flip-flops and wild Caribbean-style shorts were the attire for the evening. Prior to the night of the bash, I managed to acquire some fake tan from the chemist!

Come the night of the bash, having applied the fake tan to my visible/exposed skin, I was ready to get into the swing of it. My palms were almost glowing from the times I had applied the fake tan to my body parts. Good advice for anyone thinking of using fake tan: a) Get someone qualified to do it, b) Use rubber gloves. Gray.

Halfway through the bash, the music was silenced and either Peter or Adam gave a speech with regards to the reason behind having the bash. He then called Neil and myself forward to make presentations to us. Neil and I were both presented with mementoes from the Platoon in gratitude for our time with the Mortars. The Platoon and guests wished both Neil and I awe the very best for our futures. A toast was then given, and the music, drinking and dancing continued till 'Endex'. A great night was had by all in attendance. I truly appreciate and value the friendship of all there that night.

Cheers aye, Gray.

I was given a date to attend a two-day induction into Army life which was held at Glencourse Barracks near Penicuick. I also received a rail warrant in order to get from Inverness to Edinburgh. On arrival at Waverley Train Station, all prospective recruits were mustered onto an awaiting bus, ready to take us to the barracks in readiness for induction.

The coach dropped us off at the gym complex in Glencourse, where we were instructed to leave our luggage in a designated area, prior to receiving a brief in the changing rooms. We were all formed up in a room where we were to be addressed by members of the Depot Training Team. I remember that we were informed by a Corporal that during our 'Phase One training' – ten weeks in Edinburgh – that a film crew from Scottish Television would be filming throughout. We were also informed if anyone had any objection to being filmed, then we would be best advised to pick up our luggage and get lost out of the front gate – SIMPLICITY.

My thoughts at that precise moment were YEP! Welcome to the British Army. The accommodation that we were allocated during induction was top camp (Milton Bridge). This was the same camp where I spent my two weeks TA Recruit Court (coincidentally)!

During our two nights of induction, we had the chance to get to know each other. I met a guy called Iain MacDonald fae Ballintore (Tain). Also met a guy called Colin Smith (Smudge), he was from Stornoway. Both Iain and Smudge were joining the 'Blue Maff' same as myself. Also met a guy called Craig Learmonth who was set for joining the King's Own Scottish Borders' Regiment – KOSBIES as they were known. Other guys that were befriended were set for joining the following other fine Scottish regiments: 1st Battalion Gordon Highlanders – By DAND, The Royal Scots – 1st and Foot, 1st Battalion Royal Highland Fusiliers – The White Maff, 1st Battalion the Black Watch, The Argyll and Sutherland Highlanders.

When the induction was completed, it was a case of back on the bus to take us to Waverley train station and all our respective journeys home.

Mum was relieved and so happy to see me walk through the door; Duke was happy to see me as well. Margaret was at work. Mum couldn't wait to hear my news on how the induction had gone. I could clearly see from the look on Mum's face that she was putting on a brave front in order to mask her growing fears and concerns about me joining the regular British Army. At the end of the day, it was something that she would be required over time to learn to adapt to. Mum knew she had to respect my wishes in joining the Army. At the same time I knew I would be required to give her plenty of positive reassurance.

One of the other seasonal jobs that I had prior to enlisting into the Army was with a holiday company called HF Holidays. They had a network of hotels up and down the UK, as well as a hotel in Freshwater Bay on the Isle of Wight. I managed to secure a job as a general assistant in a hotel down in St Ives, Cornwall. I ended up in a casual relationship with a lovely lass fae Liverpool. Caroline Bills was her name. The management of the Chy Morvah were a lovely married couple by the name of Keith and Julia Clarke. Bob (true gentleman) was the Head Chef, with Paul as his 2IC. There was a guy called Alan doing Kitchen Porter. Paul's girlfriend (sorry, can't remember her name) and her sister Bev, and a wee lassie fae Manchester Faye made up the rest of the house team, with Caroline in charge.

There was a bar called Harlequins across the road behind the hotel. Caroline, Faye and I used to be regulars in there when the shift finished in the Chy Morvah.

Cornwall being famous for its amazing golden beaches was a surfers' paradise for many. I opted to try body boarding whilst working in St Ives. I remember finishing a Christmas and New Year season at the hotel, rather than going back home to Alness, I ended up going to Aldershot – Hampshire.

The reason for this was to undergo my B3 Chef's Course which was pre-planned by 2/51 Highland TA in Inverness. The course was held at the Army School of Catering in the Shot. I remember being advised by someone to avoid any pubs with the Parachute Regiment Wings emblem. Advice that was strictly adhered to! I am not in anyway being disrespectful to the Paras. I have got and always had the utmost admirable respect for each and everyone of them (past and present). Cheers aye to all 'Airborne Warriors' past and present. Gray.

If I remember rightly, prior to going to Edinburgh to commence basic training, I'm pretty sure I stopped off in Dunfermline which was where my dad was living with Sue his wife and my stepbrother Steven (who was only a baby at the time). When Dad came out of the Royal Navy after his service to HM Queen and Country, he was living in

Dirleton. Dad and Sue decided to sell up in Dirleton, and prior to buying a house in Dunfermline (Gowan Brae Drive), they were residing in married quarters in Rosyth.

I remember staying with them one time for a holiday; it was during a time when Dad got himself a job at North Queensferry Signal Station at the foot of the northside of the Forth Railway bridge. I believe my dad found it difficult/awkward when he began transition from life in the Navy to civvy street!

Dad from time to time would allow me to come to work with him. Many a time I would go exploring the rocky coastline by the Firth of Forth. I took up fishing once, not that I ever caught anything! Ah well. I attended Rosyth Navy Days on a few occasions, they were truly awesome. I remember one particular attendance that HMS *Ark Royal*, HM ships *Edinburgh*, *Andromeda*, *Fearless*, *Conqueror* (not open to the public) plus ships from HMAS – Australia and Holland were in. I met the comedian and DJ Andy Cameron onboard the flight deck of HMS *Fearless.* Respect tae you Andy. Cheers aye, Gray.

When Dad, Sue and Steven moved to Dunfermline, they ended up getting a dog called Nelson. He was a cross of some sort. I believe Dad and Sue named him as they did after Admiral Lord Nelson! I used to take Nelson out for regular walks.

The day finally arrived for reporting to Glencourse Barracks, to leave civvy street behind and enter the Military Zone. It was like going from being a boy to a man in 60 seconds! Well, okay, slight exaggeration there! Training (Phase One) was to last ten weeks based at Milton Bridge Camp.

From the moment I crossed the threshold of the barracks, life changed straight away! I don't recall much of day one, although I do remember getting issued with webbing, kit bag, combats, lightweights and all other relevant kit that we would be wearing/using during training and whilst on exercise. The webbing that we were all issued with was the '58 Pattern'. My Platoon were known as 'Balaclava Platoon'.

My training NCO was called Corporal Johnstone. "Attention to detail" was his number one quote that the Section was to become accustomed to during the next ten weeks! Much honourable and admirable respect tae Corporal Johnstone for your professionalism and instruction throughout Phase One. Cheers aye, Gray. (B. Johnstone was with the 1st Battalion Argyll and Sutherland Highlanders.) The remainder of the Training Team consisted of the following honourable instructors: Corporals Longwell – Wellie 1st Bn Queen's Own Highlanders, Stewart – Ray 1st Bn Gordon Highlanders, Middlemiss – Middy 1st Bn The Royal Highland Fusiliers. Sergeant Bryan Polson 1st Bn Queen's Own Highlanders.

The Platoon was marched down (as a squad) to the NAAFI to get the Standard Army Recruit haircut. We never had a choice in style. Everyone got the same cut. Following our trip to the barbers in Glencourse, we were all formed up again as a squad and marched back up to the accommodation blocks in top camp. Once we got fell out it was a case of into our respective billets and cracking on with our locker layouts. Corporal Johnstone was Duty NCO that night and he came round the lines to check on progress of the Platoon.

One of the first lessons we learned in discipline and respect, was that when any member of the Training Team entered the lines, immediate action was to stand to attention, until the team member gave the command 'at ease'.

When Corporal Johnstone was satisfied with the Section's progress he called for me to go with him. Once outside of the lines, he informed me that he had been looking through the files of all the members of the Section, and when he saw my file, he seemed to be impressed with my time spent as a No 2 with the Mortar Platoon in the TA.

I kind of got the impression from the Corporal that he would be looking at me being kind of a role model/mentor amongst the Section, should anyone encounter problems with weapon handling etc.

There were posters on the walls of the billet, posters with 'Markmanship Principles' on, as well as various characteristics of a military nature.

I think we eventually got lights out gone midnight, the tone of excitement about the following ten weeks of training gradually decreased until everyone was fast asleep.

The next morning the lights were switched on between five and six o'clock by Corporal Johnstone. You could tell some of the guys were not early birds… laughing out hysterically! Yip, the next ten weeks were to consist of a lot of late nights and same amount of early mornings. Welcome to life in the British Army.

The next ten weeks was to consist of a lot of physical training, fieldcraft, weapon handling, range work (at Castlelaw), first aid training, nuclear-biological-chemical training, drill, battle PT, booling brogues, regimental history, etc. Oh yes, loads of admin and room and locker and block job inspections. All essential character building and the making of future infantry soldiers.

Recruit training for the Armed Forces was designed so that it would not be a simple 'walk in the park' for recruits. It was obviously designed to create physical, mental, psychological, societal challenges for individuals willing and prepared to excel themselves in a positive and professional manner, with great feelings of pride, dignity, self-esteem and achievement. The term 'Beasting' was adopted at one point in history! The word Beasting is just an Army banter term.

Personal fitness is a key element contributing to the making of a great soldier/sailor/airman/woman. Personal fitness is also a key element of contributing to a positive well-being for any/all members of the human race.

Key elements for the making of an awesome professional member of the Armed Forces include the following :
personal pride, honesty, dignity, professional, personal attitude to overcome adversity, willingness to learn and

develop new skills, courage and strength, self-discipline, integrity, commitment, self-respect and respect for others, self-motivation, ambition.

QUALITY QUOTE: "In order to make a quality cake – you will require quality ingredients." Cheers aye, Gray.

I remember one afternoon that the Platoon had NBC lessons, the gas chamber in Glencourse had already been booked. Corporal Longwell (Welly) improvised, adapted and overcame! He had a 12-man tent rigged up, thus enabling the Platoon to carry out NBC drills (with the use of CS tablets).

The Platoon was put into groups of six, each group donned NBC suits carrying respirators round the waist. Prior to a group entering the improvised chamber, they were to carry out masking-up drills. By the time my group went in, I was reflecting on what we had been taught/instructed in previous lessons. Once inside the tent and after it was sealed up, Welly got us walking in a clockwise direction (circle), he then informed us what was going to happen.

We were going to carry out canister-changing drills, which entailed the 'Blot-Bang-Rub' technique – using fullers earth to decontaminate. The technique involved decontamination around the hood seal, followed by removal of the canister from the mask, passing the canister around the back of us, then reapplying back to the mask (respirator). The blowing out hard when putting canister back on.

Once everyone had completed the drills, Welly then informed

us that one by one we would be asked to remove the respirator prior to exiting the tent. When my turn came around, I will admit I was a little apprehensive about what was coming! Once my respirator was off, I got a taste of the CS (YUCK!). Welly then asked me my name, rank, number and who was the Colonel in Chief of the Queen's Own Highlanders. I managed to blurt the answers out prior to being ushered out of the tent. (Colonel in Chief of the Queen's Own Highlanders was His Royal Highness Prince Philip, The Duke of Edinburgh.)

I remember the Platoon being up on the Pentlands one day. We were given a scenario that a military helicopter had downed in the area and that we had been tasked to patrol out to the site, administer first aid to any casualties prior to extracting from the area with the wounded. This was training and not a real-life scenario. Once we had located the crash site, we set about administering first aid to the casualties. During the task in hand, there was a film crew/unit from Scottish Television filming us. I remember this well, as when I finally got to watch the footage I was seen dragging a wooden gate (which was intended to be used as an improvised stretcher). That idea was soon abandoned after I fell in a small hole with the gate on top of me. In the end, the Section opted to use ponchos as improvised stretchers. Must have been a good laugh for all that watched the programme when it was aired on TV.

The idea behind that exercise would have been for the Training Team to assess many things of which included the following: team work as a Section, leadership, individuals initiative and first aid skills.

I enjoyed all aspects of training. As an individual it taught me discipline, morals, respect, compassion and self-control as well as using my initiative.

I remember the time when the Platoon had our first insight in fieldcraft – building/erecting shell scrapes, bashas in a harbour area, putting up comms cord for night use.

Our first insight into 24-hour ration packs was awesome! The Training Team gave a great demonstration on the contents of an individual 24-hour rat pack. The Platoon gathered round to see what we could expect to find in our packs after the demo was finished!

One by one the contents were taken out of the demo pack, boil-in-the-bag meal, biscuits brown, cheese spread, condiments pack consisting of tea, coffee, Bovril, sugar, milk powder, chewing gum, water purification tablets, boiled sweets, fruit biscuits (hard tack), chocolate and porridge oats. When the NCO doing the demo opened up the condiments pack he pulled out a five-pound note and a 20 pack of cigarettes (much to the surprise of all the smokers in the Platoon!). Then he pulled out a pack of fresh bacon and a bottle of Becks! When the demonstration was complete, the Platoon bomb-bursted back to their respective bashas to explore their ration packs!

All you could hear in the harbour area was "Have you got your fags Min" as well as "I've nae got my money or Becks". Of course the NCOs were in hysterics by this time; they had pre-planned the demo for a laugh with the cigarettes, Becks, five pounds and the bacon. Morale building in its finest form. LOL.

At one point during training, there was an opportunity for families to come and visit the recruits. Mum was not a great traveller so she never came. Dad and Sue came over from Dunfermline. The visit boosted morale greatly. I was so glad to see Dad and Sue, I was able to tell them how training was going and also how much I was looking forward to passing out at the end of the ten weeks. Dad brought me a little statue of a duck with a Rambo-style look about it. It had a little plaque at the base with the wording 'I survived the Beasting'. (Beasting was not an un-humanitarian term, it was Army banter for intense training.)

On another occasion during training, following a big OC's inspection (Officer Commanding) the Platoon were given a long weekend. Myself and Iain (Boc McSpooch) both stayed in Edinburgh. We went into town one afternoon, had a couple of beers and something to eat. We ended up talking to a couple of lassies from Italy. I exchanged addresses with one.

When the weekend was over, the focus at the forefront of the recruits' minds was to get through the last couple of weeks prior to a proud passing out day for both recruits and family and satisfaction of the Training Team.

I remember having been on an exercise, I had just come off a two-hour stag (the weather was cold and wet). It was night-time, so I used the comms cord to guide my way back to my basha. I managed to get my Gore-Tex jacket and trousers off with the minimum fuss/noise and then got into my doss bag (sleeping bag). I was just getting comfortable and ready to drift off to sleep when I heard a Land Rover pulling up at the edge of the wood/harbour area! I was on the verge of falling asleep when all of a sudden I heard someone outside of my poncho. At this a voice asked, "And who do we have in here then?" By the tone of his voice, I was able to guess that the visitor was an officer. I responded with my rank and name, and at this the officer made himself known. He was 2IC of the Scottish Division. He never stayed for long, just long enough to ask me how morale was. I responded with morale was good.

During the last two weeks at Milton Bridge, some new faces were noticed around camp, in the cookhouse and in the NAAFI. They were recruits on TA basic training. I was a little surprised as some of them were female. (I am not being sexist when I write this.) I remember from my recruits course with the TA there was no female recruits back then. I suppose the times were changing. The last two weeks were spent brushing up on drill as well as a lot of individual personal pride with booling brogues.

Prior to the passing out parade, the Platoon had a tactical exercise including an enemy (the TA recruits).

I remember the final exercise very well, the Platoon had been bugged out from our Harbour area, we had to don full NBC kit, prior to commencing a TAB (Tactical Advance to Battle) over the Pentlands. The TAB was hard going in the dark in full NBC kit;, the way I looked at it, we weren't going to be in the kit forever. Our FRV (Final Rendez Vous) point was at the bottom of a steep hill. Once we dekitted from NBC attire we were briefed on the final advance (uphill) to capture enemy positions.

When the order was given, we proceeded to move uphill in our respective sections. We must have advanced three quarters of the hill when we began to see the shadow of the treeline at the top, At that point, a 'Shamoolie' went up from the trenches of the enemy, then all hell broke loose – silence was shattered as orders were shouted out and the sound of blank ammunition engulfed the early morning silence.

By this time, adrenalin levels were hitting high port as the Platoon advanced to the enemy trenches and took control of them as well as their occupants.

Once the Platoon had run over the trench systems, ENDEX was shouted out by the Training Team, thus resulting in a mixture of relief, sighs and overall satisfaction amongst the Platoon. By this time, daylight was blessing everyone with its presence, and by now everyone was mucking in to pick up as many of the spent blank rounds (brass).

Once we had all been debriefed and had all given our declaration that "Sir, I have no blank rounds or empty cases, pyrotechnics or parts thereof in my possession, Sir" it was onto the four tonners (Bedford lorries) and back to Milton Bridge to undertake weapon cleaning and admin following the exercise.

That night the Platoon had a 'smoker' (a social get-together) in the NAAFI. When we arrived in the NAAFI, we were greeted with a large inflatable bungee run! The TA recruits were having their smoker same time as ours, so it was (figure of speech) a very sociable night. I ended up speaking to a lovely lassie from Falkirk by the name of Alison.

The next day was very much one of admin, packing up our locker contents into MFO boxes in readiness for going down to Ouston from where the Platoon would be undergoing Phase Two training prior to passing out as infantry soldiers.

There was a hive of excitement in the Lines (accommodation) that night, what with having the passing out parade the following day. Final touches were made to Glengarry tails, brass belt buckles and brogues. Everyone was talking about how they were looking forward to putting on a professional parade of pride and self-achievement for families and loved ones coming to watch the parade. I was looking forward to seeing Mum and Dad and Sue. My stepbrother Steven was still a baby then.

The morning of the passing out day had finally arrived. Following breakfast in the cookhouse it was straight back to the lines to crack on with getting block jobs squared away as well as cleaning the lines in readiness for the next intake of Phase One recruits. Once the lines had been inspected by the Training Team, it was time to get changed into No 2 dress, which consisted of brogues, tartan trews, No 2 shirt and No 2 jacket and tie and Glengarry (TOS for the Black Watch). (TOS standing for 'Tam O'Shanter', alternative Scottish headdress to the Glengarry.) Queen's Own Highlanders tartan trews (trousers) was the Seaforth tartan. Each Scottish regiment had their own individual respective tartans. I believe regimental tradition/history is the appropriate term.

A display had been arranged for families and loved ones to watch and browse over prior to the highlight of the afternoon!

When it was time for the Platoon to be marched down to Glencourse to meet up with family, we all formed up on the road outside the Training Team's office, where we were inspected by Sergeant Polson and the NCOs. Once that was done the words "Platoon – Platoon Shun" echoed all around Milton Bridge Camp prior to Balaklava Platoon stepping off and marching down to Glencourse for our passing out parade.

There was a positive aura of mixed feelings of pride, joy, achievement and a great sense of dignity as the Platoon marched down to the main road and through the gates of the barracks. Families and loved ones were dotted around the edge of the Parade Square eagerly looking for their proud soldier – son, brother, father, boyfriend.

Prior to being 'fell out', the Training Team briefed us up on the format leading up to what time to be back on parade for the passing out.

On hearing the command to "fall out", the Platoon turned to the right and marched off three paces, prior to setting off in all directions of the compass in order to find their families and loved ones.

It never took too long for myself to locate Mum, Dad, Sue and Steven in his buggy. They were all elated to see me just as much as I was to see them. I asked Mum how her journey down from Inverness had been for her. Mum informed me that her coping strategy was that she had positive focus of me dressed in ceremonials, and was just so looking forward to see me passing out as a Phase One accomplished soldier. At that

I gave her a massive hug of love and reassurance. It was great seeing Dad, Sue and Steven as well. I was truly proud of Mum in the fact she had overcome her fear of travelling to make the three-to-four hour train journey down from Inverness to see the passing out.

Before long, time had come for the Platoon to get fell in with weapons and bayonets fixed. The Training Team carried out a last minute inspection, prior to hearing the pipes and drums playing a variety of marches.

Then the command came from Lt Barker, "Balaklava Platoon. Balaklava Platoon – Shun." "This is it lads – heads held high with pride and dignity" were the words of encouragement from one of the members of the Training Team. (Words that would stay with the majority of the Platoon for a lifetime.)

As we stepped off with the sound of the pipes and drums echoing around the Parade Square, the feelings and emotions that were running through my mind and body were positively overwhelming and of an immense professional high standard.

My inner most positive personal thoughts were doing somersaults in my head, as we were marching across the Parade Square in front of all the dignitaries and families and loved ones.

I don't have any recollection of whom the Inspecting Officer was that day.! Following the inspection, prizes were presented to the 'Best Recruit', 'Best Shot' and 'Best Fitness'. I never made any of the three, although my prize was simply that I was stood amongst the Platoon on that amazing day of passing out as a Phase One infantry recruit, at the same time wearing with the highest of pride, my dark blue Glengarry with its Queen's Own Highlander Cap badge and distinguished Blue Hackle. CFGB – ALBA GU BRAITH (SCOTLAND THE BRAVE). The last thing prior to marching off the Square that we undertook was a 'Review of Order'. We were brought to attention, followed by a 'shoulder arms', we then marched towards the Inspecting Officer, stood on the dias. We were halted short of the dias, which was followed up with a 'Present Arms' (offering up of arms to the Senior Officer). Permission was then sought by Lt Barker to the Inspecting Officer to march Balaklava Platoon off the Parade Square. In turn, the Inspecting Officer granted permission. Following this acknowledgment, the Platoon were given a right turn from where we marched to edge of the Parade Square, prior to being given an 'about turn'. As we drew level with the dias (on our right side) we were given an 'eyes right' a token of salute/respect to the Inspecting Officer. In turn the IO gave a salute back. Once we were given the 'eyes front', we marched off the Parade Square to a combined sound of rapturous applause from families and the sound of the pipes and drums. Prior to the Platoon being Fell Out for the last time three cheers were given to the Training Team, as well as an almighty loud one for HM the Queen.

Prior to getting changed into civilian attire, I went round the Training Team to express my sincere thanks. Corporal Longwell (Wellie) responded, "See you when I get back to the Blue Maff, Coolie."

My recollection of my two weeks leave is very minimal and hazy! I do remember spending a couple of days in Falkirk with Alison prior to spending the rest of my leave at home in Alness with Mum. The love/hate relationship that I had with my sister was still on-going during leave. One day we ended up having an argument over a minor issue. Margaret ended up getting the final words in by saying, "You won't last long in the Army. You will be in Colchester before long." (So many cruel/harsh words can so very often be expressed by individuals in the heat of the moment!) I also made a couple of memorable visits to Conon Bridge to see my Granny Hubbard.

Mum Fiona, Granny Margaret & Sister in Hong Kong

Me as a tiny toddler

My Dad, My Hero 'Rocky'

Bill and Jenny Tatnall holding the VIA Ball of Hope, Fort Grey, Guernsey

Brothers in Arms

REspect and REgards

Symbolic-Status

Breakwater - St.Peter Port Guernsey

The Cenotaph, London

Horse Guards Parade, London

Taffy H and I at No 10

News Letter

Date 13 May 2009
Page 13

ClipSEArch

COMMEMORATION: the Prince of Wales meets veterans Ted Ogle, centre, and Graham Culton, right, after a service to mark the 90th anniversary of the charity Combat Stress

PICTURE: Eddie Mulholland/PA

Charles honours charity for servicemen

BY TONY JONES

UK: The Prince of Wales joined former servicemen yesterday to acknowledge the achievements of a charity which has helped thousands of psychologically-scarred military veterans rebuild their lives.

Charles and the Duchess of Cornwall were among the congregation at Westminster Abbey for a service of commemoration, celebration and rededication to mark the 90th anniversary of the organisation Combat Stress.

The charity was founded in May 1919 in the aftermath of the World War One which left many soldiers shell-shocked and mentally damaged.

Over the following nine decades, almost 100,000 people have been helped by Combat Stress which provides short-stay clinical treatment and community outreach services.

It is caring for 4,000 ex-servicemen and women, including 265 who served in Iraq and 58 who were deployed to Afghanistan, with the youngest veterans aged just 20.

During the service the work of the charity was celebrated through hymns, prayers and readings.

The address was given by the Right Rev David Conner, Dean of Windsor and Bishop to the Armed Forces.

He highlighted how many veterans take more than a decade to seek help for the psychological problems they are suffering – on average about 14 years.

He told the congregation: "The hidden wounds they suffer are wounds suffered in our name and for our benefit – too easily we can ask too much of them."

Awesome meeting with the future King HRH King Charles III

Ex Grand Prix Kenya 2002

In the NAAFI in Bosnia 1994

Myself and HOBO

Dame Vera Lynn and Graham Culton

Cilla and Graham

Strictly-Speaking.....Anton is Treble-A

Question for 10 Points, with Bill Beaumont at Wimbledon

Going for Gold - Silver - Bronze @ the London 2012 Olympic Games

PHASE TWO INFANTRY TRAINING

Leave was gradually coming to a close. I made sure I spent some quality time with both Mum and Granny, prior to getting my stuff packed in readiness for catching the train from Inverness to Edinburgh, Newcastle then a Metro train to the Metro Centre outside of Newcastle. On arrival at the Metro Centre there was a coach awaiting the arrival of Phase Two infantry recruits, ready to shuttle us all to ITC Ouston.

I will gladly admit to this… I did have minor anxious thoughts whilst on the coach, making its meandering mileage to ITC Ouston. This anxiety was short-lived with the positive thought of 11 weeks time – I will be 'passing out' of here, and will be joining the ranks with the 1st Battalion Queen's Own Highlanders. This was a very overpowering, positive thought and the greatness of it enabled my minor anxiety to evaporate completely.

When the coach came to a halt outside of our new accommodation for the next 11 weeks, it was a simple case of 'all off the bus' (dismount). We were met by our new Training Team. From what and whom I can recall, the team consisted of members from the 1st Bn. The Black Watch and 1st Bn. of the Royal Scots and possibly 1st Bn. The Argyll and Sutherland Highlanders.

The sections were kept to the same format as we had been in whilst on Phase One. My Section's corporal was Corporal Smith fae the Royal Scots. Respect and thanks to you,

Smudge. Cheers aye, Gray. We kept the same Battle Honour – Balaklava – as our Platoon title whilst in Ouston.

Moving into Phase Two training is what I classed as positive progression. Development towards a positive career as a member of a big organisation – the British Armed Forces, a career that not every individual of the British human race was cut out for! It takes a lot to become a member of the Armed Forces – 'qualities' I feel is the appropriate term to use! Qualities that every member of the human race have personal possession of. Every individual Member of the human race are individually unique in their own individual ways! Gender, race, learning abilities contribute towards each individual's uniqueness. The fact that I had completed Phase One training with success was a great sense of achievement for me, as I imagine it would have been for all of the lads in the Platoon, as I also imagine would be the same sentiment for each and everyone whom has experienced similar achievements, whether they be with the Armed Forces or any other career. Positive development in turn will result in positive progression in life. (The alternative of this would simply be 'Negative development will result in negative regression'. Cheers aye, Gray.

Later on in the day at Ouston, the Platoon were given a guided tour of the establishment in order that we all knew where relevant buildings were, i.e. Cookhouse, Guardroom, Armoury, Medical Centre, ITC Ouston Headquarters, etc. The tour enabled us all to orientate ourselves to our new surroundings for the next 11 weeks. (Oh yes! – I can't forget to mention the 'NAAFI'!)

Following the tour, we all went (marched) round to the Quartermaster's Store to retrieve our MFO boxes containing our uniforms and kit. The rest of that day was spent sorting out locker layouts, ironing kit in the Section room.

During the next couple of weeks, everything that the Platoon undertook was a gradual build up! Regarding fitness, first aid training (both practical and theory), weapon handling, range days etc. Everyday a little bit more intensity was added to the training programme/regime. Before we knew it, our first leave had arrived. Myself and all the lads were truly looking forward to getting home to see our families/loved ones.

The day before we were stood down to go home was spent doing a variety of things including getting issued with rail warrants, block jobs and general cleaning of the lines (accommodation).

The next day the Platoon Commander had the Platoon on parade outside the lines. The Training Team were present. We were given positive advice that whilst we were on leave, to stay out of trouble with the police, remain focused for return to Ouston. Also that the training programme would be more intense than it had been in the past weeks.

Following the brief, we were all fell out and made our way to the awaiting coach ready to take us to the train station for our onward and upward journey home. Once we had exchanged warrants for train tickets, myself and some of the lads converged in the station bar for a bevy (drink).

I travelled up to Edinburgh with Ian (Boc McSpooch). When we arrived into Waverley Station we were somewhat shocked to discover that there were no more trains running that night up to Inverness. This somewhat unexpected situation left us both with a minor dilemma! I can't recall what brought us to the decision that we both agreed to. We took a walk up to Edinburgh Castle; when we reached the sentry box at the lower end of the esplanade we both realised why we had made the decisions to go up to the Castle! Stood at the sentry box were two soldiers in combats. Their awesome cap badge was only that of the Queen's Own Highlanders. RESULT – Caber Faigh Gu Braith. Boc and I explained our situation to the soldiers, from which they radioed the Guardroom to inform the Guard Commander of our minor predicament! Before long, the radio of the sentries came to life, instructing them to direct Boc and I up to the Guardroom at the entrance to the Castle.

On arrival we were greeted by the Guard Commander, (sorry can't remember your name!). Thank you for your hospitality that night. Truly and forever appreciated. CFGB. Cheers aye, Gray.

Boc and I were invited into the Guardroom, where we were offered a brew (tea/coffee); the members of the Guard on rest made us both feel so welcome. Thanks guys, truly appreciated. On discovering that Boc and I were both destined for the 'Blue Maff' on completion and passing out the guys were interested to hear how we were both enjoying training. We both replied with our individual responses, of which were both positive. We were both looking forward to passing out and getting to Battalion and getting settled into our respective allocated companies within Battalion life.

The following morning, Boc and I were awoken along with the Guard, one of the guys made us both a brew, prior to us expressing our thanks and appreciation for allowing us to doss down for the night. We then made our way back to the train station to catch the train up to Inverness.

On arrival in Inverness we made our way round to the bus station to catch the No 25 bus to Tain. Ian (Boc) was from Balintore. The bus went to Alness first, prior to continuing on to Tain. When I got to the house, Duke saw me passing the living room window, and by the time I got to the door he was already waiting to greet me. Mum at this point was in the kitchen making coffee for us both. She was so happy to see me home. We both sat down at the kitchen table and had a good chat with the odd question for each other.

I don't have much recollection of that leave period! I do remember going through to Conon Bridge a few times to vist my Granny.

There was a nightclub in Dingwall! I remember going there a couple of times, I always remember a song played by New Atlantic, 'I Know'. It was quite a catchy tune, one that I remember to date.

Before I knew it, leave had come to an end and it was time to say cheerio to Mum. Following the bus trip back to Inverness, and the train trips to Newcastle and Metro Centre, back on the coach back to Ouston. The majority of the lads were still on a bit of a high following leave. That first night back in lines I spent booling my brogues in readiness for the passing out parade at the end of training. I really took a great sense of pride when working on my ceremonials.

The remainder of time spent at Ouston entailed guard duty, battle pt, bayonet training. We were given a beasting prior to cracking on with 'Fix Bayonets – On Guard' and charging sand-filled sandbag dummies. When we had to provide a guard, the best turned out soldier prior to 'Guard Mount' was always stood down. The term for this was 'Stickman'. I managed this on two occasions, which gave me a great sense of achievement. The incentive behind the Stickman was obviously to encourage the lads to put great (extra) effort into taking pride when pressing combats and shining boots. (More so when pressing uniform/ceremonials.) It was all about taking self-pride in what we undertook as infantry soldiers.

We had a lot of range days with our personal weapons – SA80 – fitted with a 'SUSAT' – Sight Unit Small Arms Trilux.

Every time my Section had a room and locker inspection, Corporal Smith (Smudge) always had his own individual technique when entering the room! Rather than using his hand to turn the door handle to come in, he used his boot instead. Every time the door swung open, it always bounced off the side of my locker resulting in something in my locker being misplaced (hence I never got pulled up for it). I remember Smudge picking my brogues up during one inspection, he looked impressed with them, and he queried as to whether I had been using 'Clear' (floor polish). Some recruits had a tendency to use Clear on their brogues as a shortcut. There was however a downside to this 'cheats' method! Individuals that used Clear were always found out! Whenever water came into contact with brogues/boots that had an application of the stuff they tended to turn blue. (Using Clear was an option that we all had. It was personal preference whether we as individuals chose to take/use it.) Cheers aye, Gray.

I remember having my first experience of being on the grenade range! Having seen war movies prior to enlisting created an image in my mind of the destruction that a grenade could create. I will admit that I did have/encounter minor apprehension when I was called to the throwing point. This apprehension was overcome with positive impulse and belief in myself (as well as trust in Corporal Smith (Smudge)). Smudge calmly talked me through (encouraged) the process involved. When I was composed and ready, I pulled the pin, and with an overarm throw lobbed the grenade down the range. Straight away, Smudge and I took cover behind the throwing pit. It never took long before I heard the explosion and thump of the grenade detonating. Smudge asked if I was okay, and how I felt at having thrown my first grenade. I replied with one word – "AWESOME".

The final stage of the Phase Two training entailed a field exercise, involving all aspects of our combined Phase One and Two training. This was the final 'cherry on the cake' test prior to passing out and becoming a member of one of the biggest and most positive organisations going – the British Armed Forces. This was our chance to shine brightly and show the Training Team that we were ready to move into life within our respective regiments as pride-filled and confident and courageous, strengthened infantry soldiers.

During the exercise, the weather conditions were not always kind. Driving winds combined with rain created levels of negative barriers of adversity. ('If it's NOT raining, it's NOT training.") This negativity strengthened my positive focus on the goal of positive membership at the end of the adverse dark tunnel (tunnel vision!). We all as members of humanity will experience tunnel vision during our personal journey/voyage in life!

I have experienced high levels of tunnel vision throughout my own personal journey/voyage; this has been due to the high levels of negative momentum and experiences throughout my life.

Through the negative experiences I have encountered, I have always found/discovered positive strategies which in turn had counteracted the negative. This in turn has created a medium balance in my life. Life can be perceived in many ways by all individual members of humanity! What do I mean by this? We as individuals have all got individual learning abilities, attitudes, opinions, preferences, likes/dislikes, etc.

Life is by no means an easy journey/voyage for individuals 24/7! Life is not about what others make it for us. It is what we as individuals make for ourselves. Cheers aye, Gray.

During the last couple of nights of the exercise, my focus remained on that positive bright light at the end of that dark tunnel. Through that focus of looking ahead whilst concentrating on the there and then, I failed to look after my feet! I began to experience pain and discomfort with them. I was determined to see the exercise through from start to finish, endeavouring to overcome any adversity in the process.

The final phase of the exercise involved a dawn attack on a premeditated position. By this time my feet were not in a good way, yet I embraced the pain and kept my focus on the job at hand – at the same time on that bright positive beacon at the end of that mental tunnel.

It was an overwhelming and positive feeling of relief and aspired achievement on hearing the words 'ENDEX" from the Training Team. It was an awesomely amazing sight to see the sun rise that morning. Once the Platoon had carried out a sweep of the position for brass and thunderflash remains and smoke grenade casing, we all lined up to give the Platoon Commander an individual declaration of "Sir, I have no blank rounds, empty cases, Pyrotechnics or parts thereof in my possession – Sir."

By this time the 'four tonners' had arrived to take us all back to Ouston for a well-deserved cooked breakfast prepared for us by upstanding chefs of the Army Catering Corps. Truly appreciated lads and lasses. Cheers aye, Gray.

Straight after breakfast it was a case of straight back to

the lines to clean/degunge weapons, followed by personal kit. Once all rifles had been inspected by the corporals we marched round to hand them in to the Armoury.

Once back in our respective rooms, Smudge came in to inform us that we were going to be having a Platoon smoker in the NAAFI at 19:00hrs that night. We had been designated an area in the NAAFI complex for our get-together.

After lunch we were packing our kit into MFO boxes ready to be deployed off to respective regiments. We were also issued with rail warrants to get us home on leave following on from the passing out parade the following day (afternoon).

I gave my brogues a touch up and double checked the rest of my No 2s (McKenzie tartan kilt, diced hose, flashes, spats, white belt and brass buckle with Seaforth Badge on the plate, and Glengarry). It was decided by the Medical Officer on return to Ouston, that I would still pass out the next day, however I would not be in the actual parade due to my feet.

The time was 18:45 and I was stood outside the lines having a cigarette with some of the lads. There was a very positive aura amongst us, which was created by everyone's achievement in having completed our 21 weeks basic training. The feeling amongst us all was positively overwhelming.

Time had arrived to head over to the NAAFI to rendez-vous with the Training Team. It was kind of weird seeing them all in civvies as we had all been used to seeing them in combats or ceremonials for the last 11 weeks.

The Platoon had been allocated a room situated in between the shop and bar/snack area. Signs had been posted to warn others that a Platoon smoker was in progress (with bold letters stating clearly "DO NOT DISTURB"). It was no surprise that at least half a dozen wet-behind-the-ears recruits felt they were immune to the signage! The PTI (Physical Training Instructor) that had put the Platoon through all physical training was a corporal by the name of Cpl. Stewart, coincidentally he was a Queen's Own Highlander. CFGB. Gray.

What really made the smoker that night was the fact that everyone was able to relax and unwind after the last intense 11 weeks. Knowing that we were all passing out the following day was each and everyone of us in the Platoon's prize for having completed 21 weeks training to become infantry soldiers in the British Army.

I remember one memorable morning whilst at Ouston, where Craig Learmonth and myself were in getting washed and shaved. All the remainder of the Platoon must have decided to take an extra five minutes gonk (sleep)! That extra five minutes cost them all dearly! One of the corporals came into the lines, only to discover that the Platoon – minus two – were still in their scratchers (beds). Not a great start to the day for those caught out. The Corporal had them all outside in PT kit to teach them a lesson for monging in bed. Craig and myself were heading off to the cookhouse for breakfast, when they came back to the lines after their beasting session.

When the smoker was finished, we all headed back to the lines to get some sleep. We were joined by Corporal Stewart, whom was speaking to myself and the rest of the guys destined for joining the ranks of the Queen's Own Highlanders.

Once back in our respective rooms, the fizz of excitement regarding our passing out was somehow preventing the majority of the Platoon from getting to sleep. Corporal Stewart gave us a great incentive to get the head down! He said he would take us outside for a wee run around Ouston – the look on his face was enough for all to hit the sack (bed).

There was a very positive aura in the room on waking up in the morning. The Platoon were in track suit order after breakfast. The thought of families and loved ones coming to watch the passing out parade was positively pure.

With the high levels of positivity within the block, time had flown by and it was time to get changed into No 2s. Putting spats on was the only part of the routine that I tended to get flustered with. The process involved wearing a pair of sports socks, then putting our red and white diced hose on (which resembled knee-length socks with the foot cut off). The brogues went on and then the spats, they had a white strap attached to the bottom of the spats; this was to prevent the spats from moving around once they were buttoned up. Once this was achieved, our red flashes were put on the outer side of each leg – two fingers below the knee bone. These were held in place with twisters (lengths of stretchy chord with small hooks).

As with traditional Scottish traits, no form of underwear was worn under the kilt. Once the Platoon was all dressed we were called outside of the block for a final inspection by the Training Team. The Platoon then formed up on the road in readiness for marching up to the hangar. Due to the issues that I had with my feet, I took a proud swagger up to meet up with my dad and sister, as well as my then girlfriend Sonia whom I met whilst at Milton Bridge. Sonia was one of the recruits from the TA course. During the last week at Ouston, I had gone to the Metro Centre in order to buy an engagement ring for Sonia. I had planned to propose to Sonia during the parade, but had decided to leave it until we got back to Stirling after the parade. Mum never came down, as the train journey would have been too much for her.

Dad asked me why I was not on parade with the Platoon. I told him about the issues that I had encountered and overcame on final ex. Sonia was with her aunty and uncle; she couldn't stop smiling after we had managed to unravel our arms from each other.

At that point, the band started playing and the Light Infantry recruits marched into the hangar followed by Balaklava Platoon. The fact that I wasn't among the ranks with the Platoon only bothered me slightly. All that mattered to me was that I had passed training and following leave, I would be joining the ranks of the 1st Battalion Queen's Own Highlanders at Dreghorn Barracks in Edinburgh.

THE CLAN

The first night of leave was spent in Stirling with my fiancée Sonia and her family. Following the huge hype of positive great feeling after the passing out parade, I said my goodbyes to the Training Team with much thanks, appreciation and gratitude. I also thanked Dad and Margaret for coming down. In Stirling that night there was a very positive atmosphere in Sonia's relative's house. That atmosphere was further enhanced when I surprised Sonia with the engagement ring that I presented to her with all my love. I spent a couple of days with Sonia and her family, prior to heading up north to Alness to see and spend the rest of my leave with Mum and Duke. I made regular visits through to Conon Bridge to see my Granny. During my time in Alness, I took Duke out for plenty of walks (on the lead of course). I had a couple of nights down the pubs in Alness High Street catching up with friends that I had befriended at Alness Academy. I had two nights at the nightclub in Dingwall as well. Two awesome nights with amazing tuneage. One song I remember being played at the time was by a group by the name New Atlantic with a tune called 'I Know' – That was a purely positive feel great tune. One that I will never forget in a hurry. Much thanks and forever appreciation to New Atlantic and all those associated with their success. Cheers aye, Gray. Time had arrived to get myself ready for joining the ranks of one of the greatest and best regiments of the British Army, the Queen's Own Highlanders at Dreghorn Barracks in Edinburgh.

Saying goodbye to Mum had become a routine ever since

leaving home to get my own independence when I went to work at Inverewe Restaurant, prior to joining the Army in August 1993. Due to the amount of times of saying goodbye to Mum, I had, unaware to myself, adopted a positive coping strategy, knowing that I would be seeing Mum again/ speaking to her on the phone. I only had feelings of slight apprehension with regards to reporting to the Guardroom of the Queen's Own Highlanders at Dreghorn Barracks (Edinburgh).

On arrival at the Guardroom, having shown my brand new ID card to the Gate Sentry, I was directed to the 'fishbowl' (window at the front of the Guardroom). The Guard Commander made a phone call to Headquarter Company, following the call I was directed to transit accommodation where I was met by a JNCO (Junior Non-Commissioned Officer/Lance/Corporal).

Prior to joining Delta Company, myself, Ian (Boc MacSpooch), Colin Smith (Smudger) and Sean Walter were joining other companies within the Battalion. We all undertook an Induction Cadre for the first week. Corporal Billy Marr was the NCO running the cadre (course). Following completion of the cadre, we all went to our respective companies. Much thanks and appreciation to Billy Marr for your positive and professional instruction. Cheers aye, Gray. CFGB.

Prior to being shown my bed space in the lines, I was introduced to my CSM – Company Sergeant Major – as well as my Platoon Commander and my company OC (Officer Commanding).

When I got to my bed space, my MFO boxes were already there awaiting to be unpacked. I put all my kit away neatly in my lockers. I was truly enjoying my time in Battalion already. It never took me long for me to befriend fellow Jocks in the Platoon. (Can't forget the JNCOs.) There was a guy by the name of Dinger Bell – Derek, whom straight away adopted me like a wee brother. I looked up to Dinger as a big brother role model figure. Another guy that I looked up to was Will McManus – Big Will. Other guys that I looked up to were the following: Mike and Moose Duffus (Mark), Nigel MacGilvray, Brian Torbet, Steve Mitchell (Mitch), Pete Manson, Ali Macrae, Sinky, Tony Ronaldson, Tony Moore (Scouse), Stevie Cairns.

It never took me long to realise and understand the meaning of 'camaraderie', with much thanks and appreciation to all the aforementioned as well as others. Cheers aye, Gray. CFGB.

I soon found myself settled into life within the 1st Battalion Queen's Own Highlanders (Seaforth and Camerons). Every Friday morning prior to the Battalion being stood down for the weekend, the CO (Commanding Officer) had an incentive for improving well-being of every individual within the Battalion – involving fitness!

The CO had at some point on arrival in Edinburgh, following the Battalion been based in Munster, Germany, carried out a recce of the Pentland Hills. This recce route soon became known as the 'CO's Run'! A run that the Battalion would be involved in as a 'Scale A Parade'. The only individuals that never undertook the run were those on essential duties.

Following completion of the run, everyone not on duty were free to enjoy the weekend. I always stayed in Barracks during weekend stand-down. I remember being on guard duty one Saturday, Dinger was asleep on one of the bunks in the rest room, I was on the bunk on the opposite side of the room to him. We were both given a nudge for evening scoff. Whilst I was having a moment of composure, Dinger was looking directly at me from across the room. Out of the blue, Dinger called me 'Nookie Bear'! It never registered with me straight away! I was later to realise that Dinger was comparing me to Roger De Courcey's ventriloquist bear 'Nookie'. LOL. And from that day – and for the remainder of my Army career I had adopted the nickname 'Nookie Bear'.

I remember another weekend during my time with the Clan Delta. Dinger was going home to Cambuslang. He had queried as to what my plans were for the weekend. I told him that I was going to go with the flow and chill out. Dinger then invited me to come with him; I accepted his invite. That Saturday afternoon, when we got to his flat, he took me to his local social club where I was introduced to his dad and family and friends. That Saturday night we went out drinking and socialising. Dinger, sincere thanks and appreciation to your awesome self. Truly and forever appreciated. Cheers aye, Gray.

During my time at Dreghorn Barracks I discovered a friend from Alness Academy! Jim Davidson had enlisted into the QOH some time before me. Jim was a drummer with the pipes and drums. Much respect and admiration and forever friendship to you, Jim. Kind and best wishes. Gray. CFGB.

Through Jim I discovered another guy fae Alness whom was a piper with the pipes and drums! Donald McKay was in the same year as my sister at the Academy. Much respect and admiration and forever friendship to your good self, Donald. Cheers aye, Gray. Jim's older brother, John, was in the Corps of Royal Engineers. Much respect and admiration tae yourself John. Cheers aye, Gray.

* Writing about meeting Jim and Donald has created a positive reaction distraction! I am currently listening to Pink's recent released CD, 'The Truth About Love'. I have been a Pink fan since 2008. Pink once did a duet with her loving dad, Jim Moore. The song was titled 'I have Seen the Rain'. I have posted the video and lyrics to my Facebook page many a time. Much respect, love, admiration and empathy to both Pink and Jim. NOW – FOREVER – ALWAYS. True appreciation also to you both lovely people. Cheers aye, Gray. X

One of the quality traits about Army life, as I believe it is in any form of employment, is the following: work hard – play well (David Guetta).

Life with the Queen's Own Highlanders in Edinburgh was absolutely awesomely amazing. It was not always a smooth flowing river. At times there were some difficult currents to deal with! As the saying goes, 'You have to accept/take the smooth with the rough!' There are only two outlooks/perspectives on/of life from each and every member of humanity – these simply being POSITIVE and NEGATIVE. Cheers aye, Gray.

I became aware of the following positive quote by a great friend of mine, JR Versace from Brighton. Thank you for your truly valued and forever appreciated friendship, bro. Cheers aye, Gray. X

"TIME IS LIKE A RIVER... YOU CANNOT TOUCH THE SAME WATER TWICE. BECAUSE THE FLOW THAT HAS ALREADY PASSED SHALL NEVER PASS AGAIN! LIFE IS NOT A REHERSAL. ENJOY AND APPRECIATE AND VALUE EVERY DAY OF YOUR UNIVERSAL LIFE JOURNEY/VOYAGE." Courtesy of my bro JR VERSACE. FRIENDS NOW, FOREVER, ALWAYS. Cheers aye, Gray. X

When not on essential duties in Edinburgh (guard fitness exercises, castle guard ceremonial, including Royal Guard at Holyrood Palace), I was left to my own devices. Nightlife in Edinburgh was postively ambient 24/7, for many reasons it was for many individuals (students, civil servants, civilians as well as members of the Armed Forces). My favourite 'Loc Stats' at the time were the Grass Market and Lothian Road. The Grass Market was always bustling with predominantly students from individual backgrounds, gender, race, religion. The variety of bars from Irish, traditional Scottish and in general Great British bars. I remember frequenting one individual bar that was renowned for karaoke. I love karaoke. Lothian Road ran downhill onto Princess Street. I used to frequent one particular club named The Subway, and was always guaranteed a great and memorable night out there. Coincidentally speaking, there was a venue in the Grass Market also called The Subway. I remember one occasion whilst at Dreghorn, the Battalion had been appointed 'Spear Head Battalion'! This meant the Battalion was at short notice to deploy anywhere in the world should the requirement for our services have been required.

(Wednesday 15th May 2013 – Loc Stat – Miles Flat in Tidworth – Wiltshire). I am currently listening to the amazingly lovely Emeli Sande's CD, 'LIVE AT THE ROYAL ALBERT HALL'. Emeli is positively Beautiful and very passionately inspiration in my life. Thank you Emeli. Gray x.

As it was, Battalion was never deployed whilst on Spearhead. Two of my memorable memories from Dreghorn were 1) My first time on Castle Guard wearing ceremonials. People from all over the world would always make a memorable visit to Edinburgh Castle whilst on holiday. 2) A ceremonial Guard of Honour for Her Majesty Queen Elizabeth II. The fact then when I enlisted into the British Army on 23rd August 1993, I did so simply for my choice. I wanted to do something positive with my life, at the same time, I fancied the idea of travel and adventure in part of a massive professional and dignified organisation – Her Majesty's Forces. I was well aware when I signed my Oath of Allegiance to HM Queen and Country that one day I may be called upon to make the ultimate sacrifice in the name of Queen and Country. I had no requirement for second thought in signing my life away in order to contribute to withholding positive peace and protection of my monarch, her family and all of man/womankind in Great Britain, including the Channel Islands – Jersey, Guernsey, Alderney, Sark and Herm.

I remember being on guard one Sunday morning. I was on the barrier when approached by a four-tonner Bedford lorry. I approached the driver's side for two reasons, firstly to identify who the driver was, secondly to inquire the nature of his visit. Having identified himself with his ID card, he informed me that he was a member of the local TA unit. I then proceeded to lift the electric barrier, allowing entry into the Barracks. When I was lowering the barrier down, someone in the back of the Bedford shouted, "Hoi… Culton!" As I turned to see who was trying to gain my attention, I was happily surprised to discover that the person responsible was one of my cousins – Neil Douglas. We never had much time to chat as a) I had responsibilities as a member of the guard and b) Neil and his oppos were off to use the swimming pool in the Barracks.

The year was 1994 and Christmas was drawing near. I was having a browse of BROs (Battalion Routine Orders) when something of great interest caught my attention 1 Royal Highland Fusiliers were based in Fallingbostel, Germany (Fed Republic). The 'White Maff' were due to be deplying to Bosnia (Yugoslavia) for a six-month operational tour, working under the United Nations as peacekeepers. Volunteers were being sought to enable RHF to be at full strength in order to undertake whatever humane tasks lay ahead in deployment.

The next day – following first parade – I went to speak to the CSM with regards to nominating myself for the 'Boz' tour. The Sergeant Major asked me, "What are your reasons for doing so?" I responded with a positive and concise answer – that being that I wanted to gain operational experience.

Later on that afternoon, the CSM saw me on the way to the Cookhouse for scran and he called me over! He said to me, "Culton, you are only in the front door of the Battalion and already you are on your way to gaining your first medal." I smiled following him saying that and responded with, "Sir, the medal will be a bonus and that the greatest feeling about what lay ahead is that I would be one of many proud ambassadors for both the Battalion and the British Army."

The CSM appreciated my response and wished me all the very best for my tour. Prior to my flying over to Germany to join RHF in Fally, I was given pre-deployment leave which enabled me to get up to Alness to spend time with Mum and Duke, and at the same time visit my Granny in Conon. Prior to catching the train from Edinburgh Waverley up to Inverness, myself and some of the lads convened in the station bar for a couple of pints. Individual morale was quite high at this point and through the flowing banter I lost track of time! Thus resulting in missing my train! A snap decision was made to catch the train to Aberdeen. Ali Hendry from the Clan was on that one, and so we had combat company – camaraderie during the journey north east to the Granite City. Literally speaking! LOL. Spirits were high in the train as well as free-flowing (with coke and vodka)!

It was Friday afternoon on that journey tae Aberdeen (MIN) LOL! People were heading home for the weekend, looking forward to seeing family and loved ones, as well as unwinding for the weekend. I was in such a positive mood – so much so that I produced a bottle of Smirnoff vodka (that I had purchased from the family NAAFI in Edinburgh).

I was offering others that were in happy spirits a drink to get the weekend off to a good start. Before I knew it, the train had arrived in Aberdeen, so I got my luggage and de-bussed. Prior to Ali parting company, he made sure I was on the right platform for the next train to Inverness. Much thanks and appreciation for that great deed, Ali. Forever appreciated. Cheers aye, Gray. I went to get on board the Inverness-bound train when it arrived, only to be stopped by the train guard! He reckoned that I was too drunk! I tried explaining to the guard that yes, I had been having a couple of drinks prior to arriving in Aberdeen. I then attempted to inform him that I was on pre-deployment leave for Bosnia. My reasoning to him never changed his mind, and at that precise moment he gave the signal to the driver to depart.

At that I was somewhat gutted, as all I wanted to do was get home to Alness to see Mum and Duke.

All I could do in the time awaiting the arrival of the next train to Inverness was sit and be patient. Before long I was on the next train. The compartments were almost chock-a-block full of rig workers and a mixture of individuals heading home for the weekend. I managed to find a seat by one of the doors. The steward came through with the refreshments trolley, I remember buying a bottle of Budweiser. The next thing I remember was waking up in a wheelchair (provided by the Station Manager) in order that the ambulance paramedics could get me to their ambulance. At some point after finishing my Budweiser, I ended up having a blackout (knocking my head in the process!). Once I was comfortable in the ambulance, we (paramedics and I) set off on the short journey to Raigmore Hospital A&E. Much thanks, admiration and respect to those paramedics. Cheers aye, Gray.

I don't have much recollection of my time at the A&E department, however when I awoke the following morning I discovered that I had been placed in a one-bed unit for observations through the night! Prior to being discharged from the hospital, I spoke to a doctor who I clearly remember was asking me, "Do you have a problem with alcohol?" I gave a concise response in, "Yes – I have got one mouth and two hands!" I don't think that was the answer the doctor was expecting! Once I had given the doctor positive reassurance that I would be okay, I was discharged from care and made my way back to the train station (passing by Cameron Barracks en route).

When I arrived at the Red Parcel Office in the station, my luggage had been placed on a trolley with a note that read "Drunk came off train from Aberdeen. Take to A&E with concussion."

One of the part-time jobs that I had on my growing list of achievements prior to enlisting was as a kitchen porter at Cameron Barracks. My Uncle Hamish (who was working in stores at the Barracks was the one that got me the job). Much thanks and appreciation, Hamish. Cheers aye, Gray.

I felt somewhat embarrassed when I made myself known to the person on duty at the parcel office! I made my way round to the bus station to catch the 25 service bus home to Alness to see Mum, Margaret and Duke. By the time I reached the front door, Duke was patiently waiting for me. He was so glad to see me, just as I was him; Mum was in the kitchen making coffee for us both – she could read my mind like a book, bless her.

Mum as per usual was always relieved to have me at home; my presence in her company gave her reassurance and positive peace of mind that I was well and safe. Natural mother instinct for all mothers.

Duke was glad to have me back home as he knew he would get plenty of long walks up and down the Averon River. Duke and I had great rapport with one another. Margaret and I were your average brother and sister (from time to time we had a tendency to argue like cat and dog!). LMAO!

I spent the second day of leave through in Conon Bridge – precious time with my Granny. She was a lovely lady, who loved and truly valued life to the MAX. Life was extremely difficult for her when Grandad passed away. (RIP Grandad – you are forever in my heart.) Grandad last worked in an auction room in Dingwall prior to his passing on to heaven. Every time I hear the children's tale about Old Mother Hubbard, I gracefully remember my Granny with love and affection. I forever love and miss both grandparents Culton and Hubbard. They are forever in my heart and soul.

My Granny Hubbard loved cats, she was almost obsessed with ginger-coloured ones – they were her personal preference. She also loved her snooker on TV; Stephen Hendry was her 'favourite boy' as she used to call him, bless. She was also very passionate about cooking and baking. I loved her coffee-flavoured Victoria sponges, filled with coffee buttercream. Granny always had a coffee sponge (stored in a Quality Street tin.)

Before long, time had arrived for me to return to Edinburgh, in readiness for flying out to Hanover Airport in order to join 1 Royal Highland Fusiliers on ops training, prior to flying to Bosnia (Yugoslavia). It was quite a surprise and coincidence that I ended up in Mortars Support Company. My feet hit the tarmac in Hanover, along with all the other great guys (like myself) that had nominated themselves for the 'Boz Tour'.

The Mortar Platoon had 432s as their mode of transport (tracked troop carrying vehicle, with a fixed turntable like base plate fitting for the 81mm mortar). That awesome piece of kit certainly packed a punch on the receiving end of rounds fired.

I was walking across to the NAAFI one night following training, when out of the blue I heard someone shouting my name! I stopped in my track to identify who was calling me. When I turned round, my cousin Gary Cormack was walking across to meet and greet myself. (Gary was attached to 1RHF as he had decided to join the Royal Electrical Mechanical Engineers.)

Prior to flying over to Split in Croatia (*Dobra Dan/Outro* – good day/morning) we were all issued with extra individual cold-weather kit comprising of the following: Matterhorn boots, Gore-Tex mitts (inner and outer), cold-weather face mask (for extreme cold weather conditions), UN beret and badge (light-blue coloured beret), light-blue helmet cover, DPM brassard with RHF tartan patch and UN patch. When the plane touched down at Split airport, an announcement was made on the plane PA system requesting that we all kept out berets off until we were inside the terminal building. I believe this was done as an act of respect and thanks to the great regiment that we were relieving from duty following their tour. When we arrived at Vitez School (night-time) there was a hive of activity, sorting out personal kit, weapons etc. Eventually we were all allocated our accommodation for the duration of the tour. We were in four-man Portacabins with two sets of bunk beds and two metal lockers.

The next six months consisted of a variety of tasks, including the following: camp guard, quick reaction force (QRF), Hearts and Minds projects in local communities, escort duties, joint patrols with Military Police, manning checkpoints, (area cleaning in camp with a blanket of snow!) – LMAO. Thoroughly enjoyed the area cleaning – NOT. (Chuckle.)

During my six months in Bosnia, I personally experienced some positive experiences, at the same time I encountered and overcame more negative experiences including the following: physical, mental, psychological, emotional abuse. I experienced heartache and sorrow following hearing the sad news that my Granny had passed away. I love and miss you so much – NOW – FOREVER – ALWAYS. Gray x.

At the end of the tour there was a positive great feeling deep within myself about what I had personally achieved during the tour. We were relieved by the Devon and Dorset Regiment. Admirable respect to each and everyone associated with that regiment, both past and present. Strength and honour. Cheers aye, Gray.

NORTHERN IRELAND

During the tour in Bosnia, an amalgamation had occurred between two fine and unique Scottish regiments of the British Army. They were the 1st Battalion of the Queen's Own Highlanders – Seaforth and Camerons – Caber Feigh Gu Braith – and the 1st Battalion the Gordon Highlanders – By Dand. ALBA GU BRAITH. The newly formed regiment became known as 1st Battalion the Highlanders.

Following leave after Bosnia, my life journey/voyage took me to Derry/Londonderry in Northern Ireland.

The Highlanders' role in Northern Ireland was as a Roulement Battalion. We were there to support the RUC – Royal Ulster Constabulary. Following completion of our two-year tour, the Highlanders returned to the mainland to take up a new role. I, however, had other plans! I had asked for a transfer to the Army Air Corps as an Air Trooper. My transfer was turned down! At that I requested an attachment to the Army Dog Unit N.I. 'Who let the Dogs Out?' – Baha Men.

Following my Patrol Dog Handler Course as well as my PTA Course (Practical Training Assistant) – Dog Baiter, I took post at Long Kesh, from where I spent the next six months patrolling the outer wall of the notorious Maze Prison. During my time there I had control of two dogs (not at the same time). The first dog I was teamed up with was a white German Shepherd named Hobo. He was scatty as! He reminded me of the dog from the kids' cartoon *Rhubarb and Custard.* The second dog that I was re-teamed with was a long-haired Shepherd called Steel. His name was so matched to his K9 mannerism – he was literally hard as nails.

During my time at Long Kesh, I experienced more positive events than I did negative. The highlight of which was meeting and getting engaged to a lovely lassie called Brenda.

Following my time at the Maze, I went back to Melton Mowbray to undertake my Naval Vehicle Search Dog Handlers Course. The dog that I was in training with was an English Springer Spaniel bitch by the name of Jess. She was so bursting with positive energy as well as loveable and adorable.

During my course, Jess and I both established a positive sense of trust and rapport. The awesome thing about many aspects of the course, was that on my return to Ballykelly I was informed by the Chief Trainer that my search partner on up-and-coming ops/tasks would be Jess. I was very overwhelmed in a very positive feeling to hear this amazing great news.

Following Jess and my 'passing out' in front of the Chief Trainer (passing out was where Jess and I showed that we were confident and trustworthy of one another, and that we could work proficiently together as a team), we became part of 39 Brigade Specialist Dog Section at Palace Barracks on the outskirts of Belfast.

During my years at 39 Brigade, I spent much of my time

working in unison with the Naval Anti-Terrorist Unit made up from the Royal Navy and Royal Marines. HM ships that Jess and I served aboard were as follows: HM ships – *Arun*, *Blackwater-Spey*, followed later by *Cottesmore*, *Dulverton* and *Brecon*. Admirable respect and sincere thanks to all officers, senior rates and junior rates, same sentiments to the Royal Marines fae Commachio Group for your camaraderie. Truly and forever appreciated. Cheers aye, Gray. Per Mare Per Terram – CFGB.

The positive highlight of my time at 39 Brigade was when I proposed marriage to Brenda! Brenda agreed to marrying me. At that point in my life, life just seemed so positively bright and beautiful! That positivity over these two years gradually deteriorated. Various forms of abuse by individuals from the Dog Section took its toll on our marriage, eventually resulting in divorce. Through all the negative events that unfolded I short-toured myself back to the Highlanders in Catterick.

On my return back to the Battalion, I was to discover that the RSM (Regimental Sergeant Major) was my former Company Sergeant Major from my time in Delta Company – Queen's Own Highlanders at Dreghorn Barracks in 1994.

Prior to my medical discharge from service on the 19th January 2003 (reason for discharge – 'Queen's Regulations 1975 para 9.387, Ceasing to fulfil Army medical standards'), 'Military Conduct on discharge – EXEMPLARY'.

During my nine years – 150 days service I served in the following: United Kingdom, Canada, Kenya, Germany. I served on operations in Northern Ireland as well as the former Republic of Yugoslavia. I was awarded the UNPROFOR medal, General Service Medal (1962), the Queen's Golden Jubilee Medal and the Accumulated Campaign Service Medal for operations in Northern Ireland.

During my tour in Derry/Londonderry in 1996, I sadly lost my mum to mental ill health. For many years of her life, my mum courageously fought two long-running battles with post-natal depression as well as bipolar disorder.

The one positive trait that I embrace passionately since her passing is simply that in my mind, Mum is no longer suffering from her mental anguish and demons from her past. I know that my mum was an extremely brave and courageous lady in her time. She did many great and positive deeds for many others in the hope of overcoming severe adversity. Mum, I sincerely miss and forever love you. I am eternally thankful to you, NOW – FOREVER – ALWAYS. Gray xxx

CELINE DION – 'I REMEMBER L.A.'

Following my medical discharge from military service in 2003, I sadly lost my dad to cancer. My dad was and still is my life hero. A 22-year Royal Navy Falklands Veteran. Dad, I sincerely miss and forever love you. I am eternally thankful to you, NOW – FOREVER – ALWAYS. Gray xxx

MIKE AND THE MECHANICS – 'THE LIVING YEARS'

CAREER SUMMARY

October 2012 Two weeks Sales Assistant at SPORTS DIRECT Guernsey, Channel Islands. Massive positive shout tae Si and awe the amazing team. LOVE YOU GUYS THE WORLD OVER. Gray.

August–Sept 2012 I was employed by CPUK as a Fire Marshal at the 2012 London Olympic/Paralympic Games. I worked on varied venues including GREENWICH EQUESTRIAN, WOOLWICH BARRACKS (OLYMPICS), ATHLETES' VILLAGE where I was a member of 1st Fire Response team to the London Fire Brigade. I held position of Manager/Supervisor on a number of occasions during my contract. Duties included patrolling all areas of Athletes' Village, venues, responding to fire alarms, carrying out fire risk assessments.

2008–2010 Sigma Group (Guernsey) Warehouse Operative, picking-packing orders, stock control, taking delivery of new stock as well as checking items in.

2006–2008 RG Falla Construction (Guernsey). Worked on various projects around the Bailiwick including Royal Court Building – medical staff accommodation, project at Admiral Park – New School Build Project. General site labour. Site security.

2006 F. Watson & Sons (Guernsey). Labourer, varied projects.
2005–2006 Steel Fixer's Labourer, Charlie Kingsman.

Various site projects, setting and fixing steel foundations.

2004–2005 Reg Bullock (Stonemason), Labourer for granite work on various projects in/around Guernsey.

2003 Barman at the Rocquettes Hotel – Tartan Bar, Guernsey. General bar duties maintaining customer satisfaction. Massive shout-out to Mr Callum Le Noury for your awesome hand of camaraderie and the opportunity that you offered myself during the early stages of my transition from military to veteran life. Truly and forever appreciated. Gray.

23rd August 1993–19th January 2003 (Infantry) Private Soldier serving with 1st Bn Queen's Own Highlanders/1st Bn Highlanders.

12-FEB-2002	KENYA
04-DEC-2000	GREAT BRITAIN
20-OCT-2000	NORTHERN IRELAND
18-JULY-2000	GREAT BRITAIN
23-JUN-2000	NORTHERN IRELAND
13-JAN-2000	GREAT BRITAIN

RECORDS HQ/MGT SVCS 11-NOV-1997
NORTHERN IRELAND 11-NOV-1997
GREAT BRITAIN 11-SEP-1995
CANADA 08-JUN-1995
NORTHERN IRELAND 15-MAY-1995
GREAT BRITAIN 02-MAY-1995
GERMANY (FED REPUBLIC) 13-NOV-1994
YUGOSLAVIA 19-SEP-1994

GERMANY (FED REPUBLIC) 1 QO HLDRS
23-AUG-1993
GREAT BRITAIN

QUALIFICATIONS ACHIEVED SINCE SECONDARY SCHOOL:

1) O'GRADE GEOGRAPHY-ENGLISH. STANDARD GRADE MATHS

2)	27-SEP-93	MILITARY SWIMMING TEST
3)	23-SEP-95	R SIGS REGULAR RADIO USER CADRE
4)	09-JUN-97	DOG HANDLER INFANTRY PATROL
5)	07-NOV-97	NAVAL VEHICLE SEARCH DOG HANDLER
6)	18-JUL-00	UNIT PHOTOGRAPHY
7)	11-JUL-00	TEAM MEDIC CADRE
8)	23-JUL-01	MESS STEWARD – BASIC
9)	20-JUN-12	MARITIME SECURITY OPERATOR

MCA STCW 95 FIRE PREVENTION AND FIRE FIGHTING
MCA STCW 95 PERSONAL AND SOCIAL RESPONSIBILITY
MCA STCS 95 ELEMENTARY FIRST AID
MCA STCW 95 PERSONAL SURVIVAL TECHNIQUES
RYA MARITIME RADAR USERS CERTIFICATE
RYA SHORT RANGE VHF LICENCE
PIRACY AND VESSEL HARDENING MODULE
MARSEC HOSTILE MEDIC (FIRST AID AT WORK/

OXYGEN & DEFIBRILLATION CERTIFICATE)
SEAFARER MEDICAL CERTIFICATE (ENG1)

10) 07-AUG-12 HABC LEVEL 2 AWARD IN FIRE SAFETY (QCF)

11) 07-AUG-11 TQ WORKFORCE DEVELOPMENT 10013787 ADULT LITERACY – LEVEL 1, 10013611 ADULT NUMERACY LEVEL 1

12) 26-NOV-11 CONSTRUCTION SKILLS HEALTH AND SAFETY (OPERATIVES CATEGORY)

13) 23-APR-10 CERTIFIED PRACTITIONER OF NEURO LINGUISTIC PROGRAMMING

14) 23-APR-10 CERTIFIED PRACTITIONER OF TIMELINE THERAPY™

Through my writing of *See Me For Who I Am,* one of my personal aims is to quash the myth that individuals suffering in silence with mental ill health are less intelligent than individuals NOT affected. In simplistic form, mental health simply means 'Matters of the Mind'.

We as individuals of the human race, have all got varied levels of intelligence from which we have obtained (educated) ourselves from our own pasts (upbringings).

Events have unfolded during my life in the past, where at the time of happening, I have not always been aware of the reason(s) for events. These reasons in my belief have been offset due to being unaware of an underlying issue in my life! The reasoning for aforementioned events have gradually become apparent through the onset of my gradual development and growth in life.

Everything happens in life for a reason! We may not necessarily know at the time why. The reason(s) will gradually become clear in time! At times when least expected! Cheers aye, Gray.

For all the negatives in life… the positive will shine through brightly.

It has taken many negative events to occur in my life… in order for the positives to aspire!

I became aware of the word 'aspire' whilst working as a Fire Marshal at/during the London 2012 Olympics and Paralympic Games. (ASPIRE v. have a hope or ambition). I also became aware of the word 'inspire' at the same time. (INSPIRE v. to stimulate to activity; encourage a feeling; cause to feel uplifted.) I was truly inspired by many of the athletes during the Olympics, however I was inspired more so during the Paralympic Games.

I cannot possibly begin to express the enormous great and positive feelings that I felt/experienced during my contract at London 2012 through expression with words so I will endeavour to share my experiences through photographic images. What really made my very memorable and positive experience at London 2012 so special, motivational and inspirational was meeting so many awesome members of the human race. Being surrounded by so many courageous and determined individuals from all around the world, was a truly immense and forever memorable experience. I give my sincere thanks and appreciation to all those that I crossed paths with.

I Graham Robert Culton hereby pay homage to every individual that I have been blessed with meeting during my 38 years as a member of Humanity. NOW – FOREVER – ALWAYS. Cheers aye, Gray.

Quality Quote

"Never allow yourself to be distracted from what matters most in life – **YOURSELF**" Cheers aye, Gray.

ALWAYS BE PREPARED FOR THE UNEXPECTED!

I Graham Robert Culton am not weird! I am wonderful. I am not mad! I have simply been misunderstood. I am not arrogant – I am awesome. I respect and love myself more now than I have ever done in the last 38 years. In turn, I only respect, admire and love those that share my sentiments. I have done more right in life than I have wrong. I shall NEVER change my own personal 'wonderous' ways for anyone. I will however change my personal perspective (outlook) on life in a positive, dignified and bright and humane professional manner. Cheers aye, Gray.
(20th April 2013)

"EVERY MINUTE OF ANGER IN LIFE DENIES YOU 60 SECONDS OF TRUE HAPPINESS!" (Courtesy of the 'L'Islet Spice Bunny' via Richard Harding from 'Islands FM – 104.7 FM')

I have spent far too long looking in my life rear-view mirror than I have been looking at the road ahead! This has resulted in myself passing many positive opportunities. Cheers aye, Gray.

BRITISH SOLDIER'S CREED

I am a British Soldier and a Warrior.
I will train hard – fight hard and think hard.
And I will do so with Courage.
I will fight for my Comrades, Commanders and the Queen.
And I will do so with Pride.
I will defeat the enemy through my Professionalism and Skill.
And I will do so with 'Self Discipline'.
I will earn the Trust and Respect of Fellow Warriors.
And I will do so with Honourable Actions.
I will Lead and Mentor All those who fight with me.
And I will serve them with Integrity and Commitment.
I will Overcome Adversity and Fear.
And I will Help others to do so.
I will Never Forget those Who have Gone before Me.

I WILL ALWAYS BE A BRITISH SOLDIER

A VETERAN 09-02-2013

Some might say that I walk – Like a Soldier walks!
Some might say that I talk – Like a Soldier talks!
Some might say that I behave – Like a Soldier behaves!
Full of PRIDE-DIGNITY-RESPECT with a Professional Mannerism.
Some might say that I dress – Like a Soldier dresses!
Of Smart and Clean turnout!
A Soldier is someone that is ready to face whatever Life may throw at him/her!
A 'VETERAN' is All of the Above – Someone whom once was a Soldier.

G. Culton
B Tatnall
(1st Bn Queen's Own Highlanders)
(Royal Signals)
CFGB

When I was attending Alness Academy. I had a part-time job working as a dishwasher at the Shoba Tandoori restaurant on Alness High Street. I was paid £5 per shift and always got a curry at the end of the shift. Much respect and thanks to Syed and Pyra – truly appreciated. Cheers aye, Gray.

Much thanks and respect and appreciation to Derek Gray for your friendship as well as getting me the job. Kind and best wishes to your awesome self and family. Cheers aye, Gray.

During the last 18 years of my life I have had many relationships with lovely ladies all over the UK and Guernsey! I have been engaged twice and married and divorced once. I met Brenda when I was attached to the Army Dog Unit, Northern Ireland. Brenda's loving family accepted me with open arms, as well as making me feel so welcome and loved. Brenda and I were married in a church in Lisburn (Co. Antrim). We were both given an amazing start as Mr and Mrs Culton. This start was made more so with the sincere and truly appreciated gift given to us both by Brenda's parents – Pat (PJ the DJ) and Maureen. They gave us the deposit that enabled Brenda and I both to purchase a house. (If my memory serves me correctly I was 23 years old when we got married.) During the two years that Brenda and I were married, I was employed as a Vehicle Search Dog Handler with 39 Brigade Specialist Dog Section at Palace Barracks. I spent much of these two years on operations (maritime-based) with the Naval Anti-Terrorist Unit, working alongside the Royal Navy and Royal Marine Commandoes from Commachio Group (45). There were two other handlers with the same job description as myself. The rota should have been a continuous cycle of one week on patrol and two weeks back in Palace. This was not the case for me as I spent more time at sea on search ops than I did back on dry land!

Of the two other handlers, one was a Lance Corporal in the Royal Engineers and the other was a Lance Corporal from the Royal Logistics Corps (Chef). The two individuals had a tendency to 'abuse' their individual positions of authority during my attachment to 39 Brigade. Their negative and abusive actions in turn created a negative reaction and emotional and psychological and mental strain on my well-being, which in turn created a chain reaction of negative events relating to my marriage.

My ex-wife suffered from several miscarriages through all the stress created by the two individuals abusing their position of authority in the Brigade.

During my time at 39 Brigade I served on board the following HM ships – *Arun*, *Spey*, *Blackwater*, *Cottesmore*, *Dulverton* and *Brecon*. I spent most of my time on board *Arun* prior to her decommission to the Brazilian Navy. She was an awesome ship to have had the great experience to have served with. Much respect and admiration to all of the officers, senior rates/junior rates and all of the 'Hoofin Lads' that I was both honoured and privileged to have worked in unison from Commachio Group – 45 Commando. SALUTE AND RESPECT. The 'Royals' adopted my search dog (Vehicle Search) Jess as one of their own. Just goes to show that Royal Marines have got a heart of gold; that goes with the 'Lean Green Fighting Machine' image that they have. PER MARE PER TERRAM. Cheers lads. Gray.

DIARY OF EVENTS

The following memoirs are from a diary that I started writing on 1st September 2006:

Fri 1st Sept 06 10am meeting Adam Farish (NCH).

Weds 6th Sept 06 Meeting with John Webb (Drug Concern) 3pm @ 'Orchard House' St Martins.

Thurs 14th Sept 06 Meet with Hannah Bayman (BBC Spotlight) (10am) Back of Brockside. Held first Awareness meeting of Making a Difference! @ 'St Martins Community Centre. 14 personnel in attendance. Meeting started 19:30 – finished @21:00 (positive response)

Fri 22nd Sept 06 (10am) Spoke to a lovely lady by the name of Gillian; Mental Health Foundation regarding 'National Inquiry Conference into Self-Harm Among Young People'. (6th Oct 06) @ 'Royal Society' in Edinburgh. Had a very positive feeling after speaking to Gillian.

Tues 26th Sept 06 Phoned Ms Marsha Parsons (MHF – Glasgow Office) regarding registration for the National Inquiry Conference.

Weds 27th Sept 06 10am meeting with Wendy and June @ Info Exchange. Thanks to both lovely ladies for their valued time. Coffee with Kim'and Dom @ Decaff.

Thurs 28th Sept 06 Having been shortlisted for the 1st

part of selection for Guernsey Fire and Rescue Service, I have decided that I would not be able to commit to both the Fire Service and Making a Difference (MAD) LOL @ this I am committing to (MAD) – priority.

Tues 3rd Oct 06 Richard Harding from Island FM phoned me to query the possibility of doing a live phone interview regarding what MAD was all about.

Weds 4th Oct 061 6:00 meeting with Sue Fleming (Senior Management – Guernsey (M.H.T.)). Offered support and backing for MAD. Thanks for your time Sue. Truly appreciated.

Thurs 5th Oct 06 I flew up to Edinburgh to attend the National Enquiry Conference. A huge THANK YOU to the amazing individuals who made it possible for me to fly to Edinburgh as well as my accommodation whilst there – They know who they are. APPRECIATED.

Fri 6th Oct 06 Felt somewhat emotional on the morning of the Conference due to personal reasons! I need to remember to get Blaize a 'Hearts' strip before I make my return journey back to Glorious Guernsey on Saturday 7th. (I promised my Little Princess that I would get her a strip.) And I did exactly as I promised, as well as getting her a mini Hearts scarf. Time had arrived to head round to the Royal Society (not even five minutes away from my hotel.) After having a cigarette I walked through the double doors of the venue to be greeted by some very friendly and welcoming faces (individuals from the Mental Health Foundation).

Much thanks and appreciation to you all for making me feel so welcome. Through attending the Conference I met a lot of amazing new contacts. The names of those that I remember are:

1) Catherine McCloghlin (CBE)
2) Dr Marcia Brophy
3) Adam Ingram – (MSP)
4) Isabella Goldie – (MHF)
5) Marsha Parsons – (MHF – Glasgow Office)
6) Andrea M Mayrhofer – (Robert Gordon University, Aberdeen)
7) Fiona Mitchell – (Barnardo's)
8) Geoff Huggins – (Scottish Executive)
9) Dr Andrew McCulloch – Chief Executive – Mental Health Foundation

For all of the names mentioned above as well as everybody else I met at the Conference – I have got the utmost respect and sincere admiration for your dedication and commitment through the inspirational work you do and continue to do so – in order that one day – the STIGMA attached to mental health will be NO MORE. THANK YOU ALL from my heart. Cheers aye. Gray.

Sat 7th Oct 06 After getting my feet firmly fixed back on Glorious Guernsey ground (Guernsey Airport) I got back to my room @ Brockside (top of the Grange, by the traffic lights). No time to unwind after my journey back from Edinburgh, Gatwick, Guernsey. I have got Blaize to stay for the night and I am totally looking forward to seeing and being with my Little Princess after my trip away to ALBA (Scotland).

Blaize has made a massive difference in my perspective of life."
Blaize... I love you NOW – FOREVER – ALWAYS.
DADDY. X

Sun 8th Oct 06 Wrote a letter to Prime Minister Tony Blair!

Mon 9th Oct 06 Posted letter to the PM. Received a call from Roisin Gauson (from *BBC Spotlight*). C.I. Roisin phoned regarding MAD at the same time she brought to my attention that the 10th October was World Mental Health Day. THANK YOU Roisin, much respect and admiration to your lovely self. Cheers aye, Gray.

Tues 10th Oct 06 WORLD MENTAL HEALTH DAY. Roisin came to do an interview (was shown on *BBC Spotlight* at half six (18:30hrs). Nice one Roisin! I was highly impressed with your fine professionalism and work. X

Fri 13th Oct 06 Had a 2 o'clock appointment with Dr Alison Kelly @ Castel Hospital. Had to cancel!

Mon 16th Oct 06 Meeting with Steve Mahy (Director of the Samaritans Guernsey). Much thanks, respect and admiration to Steve and everyone involved with the Samaritans. Truly appreciated. Cheers aye, Gray.

Tues 17th Oct 06 Meeting with Tim Redbridge (Chairman of Guernsey Mind). Much thanks and appreciation for your time. Cheers aye, Gray.

Thurs 19th Oct 06 12:00 Meet with Dr David Jeffs (Director of Public Health) and Yvonne Le Page (Manager of Human Resources). THANK YOU BOTH SO MUCH FOR YOUR TIME YOU BOTH OFFERED ME. HIGHEST RESPECT AND ADMIRATION TO YOU BOTH.

Received a letter from Ms V Gould (Scheduling Manager for the Prime Minister). Thank you for taking the time to reply to my letter to the PM'– dated '8th October 2006.

Mon 23rd Oct 06 Posted self-harm literature to Ms Elaine Jackson c/o Hautlieu School in 'Jersey. Literature sent regarding an Art Exhibition in Jersey in February 2007. Much thanks and admirable respect to your lovely self Elaine. Cheers aye, Gray.

Thurs 26th Oct 06 (14:15 hrs) @ Guernsey Police Headquarters for a meeting with Chief Officer of Police, George Le Page. Much respect – thanks and appreciation for your valued time, sir. Cheers aye, Gray.

Fri 27th Oct 06 Sent Mike Smith @ Runrig Office a Making a Difference polo shirt. Much thanks – respect and admiration to your braw self, Mike. Cheers aye, Gray.

Letter sent to Mr R Finch @ Royal Court. Much thanks, respect and admiration, sir. Cheers aye, Gray.

Fri 3rd Nov 06 08:30 Meeting with Mr Trevor Wakefield @ College of Further Education. Much thanks to your awesome self for your time, Trevor. Truly and always appreciated. Cheers aye, Gray.

Mon 6th Nov 06 Overnight sailing on the MV Commadore Clipper (Condor Ferries) to Portsmouth (POMPEY-WEY-HEY). Much thanks and valued appreciation and respect to the Captain, officers and all crew. Cheers aye, Gray.

Tues 7th Nov 06 Came off the Clipper booted and suited (wearing all of my medals). Caught train up to London Waterloo to attend Combat Stress – Armistice Lecture @ Whitehall (Venue 0 The Royal United Services Institute for Defence and Security Studies). Never got to attend the Lecture! However I did have a brief discussion with the Director of CS. Nice gentleman. Took photographs of the London Eye as well as Big Ben' During my time @ the Old War Office building I became aware of an Al Qaeda terrorist that was on trial that day for planning carnage, bloodshed and butchery on a colossal and unprecedented scale. I felt so proud of myself to be wearing my medals with so much dignity, courage and pride.

On my way back to Waterloo Station, I passed by the entrance to 10 Downing Street. I asked one of the Metropolitan Police officers whether it would be possible to get my photo taken by the renowned No 10 door! I was informed by the said officer that it wasn't a good time. Much thanks and respect to that officer and the Metropolitan Police overall. Cheers aye, Gray.

I caught the train back to Portsmouth in order to catch the

FastCat ferry across to Ryde in the Isle of Wight. Stayed with Rik and Nicky Dudley in 'Cowes for the night. (First met them in Guernsey 2004/05.)

Weds 8th Nov 06 Rik gave me a shout at 6 o'clock. Cheers mate, appreciated, After getting washed and shaved, I got all my kit squared away and went through to the living room, where I had a coffee and chat with Rik, prior to him driving me back to Ryde to catch the FastCat back to Pompey. Much thanks to both Rik and Nicky for your hospitality – truly and forever appreciated. Cheers aye, Gray.

Much thanks and appreciation to the two National Express coach drivers who very kindly gave me a lift from the Hard to the Continental Ferry Port in order that I could catch the Commodore Clipper back to Glorious Guernsey. Truly appreciated. Cheers aye, Gray.

Whilst on board the Clipper, I had a very pleasant chat with Ms Tracy Gilbertson (Customer Services Officer.) Much thanks and appreciation for your time, Tracy. Cheers, Gray.

On arrival into St Peter Port, Guernsey I went outside for a cigarette. Blaize's Mum took her down to meet me, I felt very emotional seeing Blaize waving to me and smiling.

On arrival inside the terminal, all foot passengers were greeted by a Customs and Excise Officer and Search Dog. Much commendation and admiration to both, on the way the team executed their duties in a highly professional manner – much respect and admiration to all members of

Customs and Excise/Border Agency staff. Cheers aye, Gray. Prior to going through to arrivals, I was stopped by CID! (I never had any photo ID on me, due to awaing delivery of my new biometric passport.) After CID had finished with me, I was able to go through to arrivals, and a very loving and welcome cuddle and kiss from Blaize.

On arrival back to my room at Brockside (top of the Grange) I went through to the office to check for mail. Coincidentally my new passport had arrived. Much thanks and appreciation to both Ken (RIP) and Karen Mortimer, Guernsey Royal British Legion Branch. Cheers aye, Gray.

Sat 11th Nov 06 Helping out with the Royal British Legion Poppy Appeal today. I need to meet up with Mr and Mrs Payne at Millbrook Jewellers on the Bridge – St Sampsons. Another brilliant opportunity to wear my suit and medals, whilst doing something positive for the Legion, which in turn will help/assist other Armed Forces veterans and their families.

Some may say that I am a highly opinionated person! Well they wouldn't be wrong! Considering the life experience(s) I have encountered. Cheers aye, Gray (Friday 8th Feb 2013).

The following is my own personal thought: Life is a journey/ voyage for discovery for us all as individuals in the human race. It is by no means straightforward plain sailing! From time to time we are often faced with stormy weather – life challenges and adversity. These challenges can have a negative affect during the course of our journey/voyage thus creating our mind bearings (thought process) to slip, this resulting in an alteration to our individual voyage. There are only two ways to deal with these challenges! Those being by either a) positive attitude/manner and b) negative approach. Life would be so boring were it to be all plain sailing. It has taken extreme amounts of adversity in my past life to occur in order for me to get so far in life.

It has taken for negative events to have occurred in my life in order for POSITIVE to ASPIRE. Cheers aye, Gray.

Life is for living... there are no second chances at it! I have been held back in life for far too long now by negative events (anchors). I have been gradually dropping my anchors one by one!

I – through my own personal Life experiences, and also through my own eyes – have witnessed many individuals that treat life as if it were a big competition! What do I mean by this? Simplistically, what I refer to is there is a percentage of individuals on the human race' that believe they are perfectionists! Individuals that feel thcy are more dominant than others! Individuals that feel bullying, manipulation, lying, deceit, animosity, hostility, creating heartache and sorrow for other humans is appropriate behaviour – once again in my eyes these said individuals are totally inhumane. Cheers aye, Gray.

Through all the forms of abuse that I have been subject to since childhood (when I say 'forms' I am referring to the following – physical, mental, emotional, social) from many individuals,

I have always managed to adopt coping strategies to enable myself to overcome the aftermath from the abuse. At times I have looked for a distraction! My symptoms of complex post-traumatic stress disorder have somehow become delayed through my autism.

Tues 2nd Oct 12 Sat outside Café Délices (in market area of St Peter Port). Comparing my life at present moment in time, with my glass of latte! (Full.) All good, life full of warmth and so much positivity. Life may not be 100% at present, and only I know what I have to do in order to achieve that complete percentage. I shall endeavour to not allow others to hinder my personal beliefs and direction in life. ONWARDS and UPWARDS. Cheers. Gray. I would like to say a massive thank you to Bertrand and his awesome team at Café Délices. I truly appreciate and value your friendship and services offered. Cheers aye, Gray.

Weds 3rd Oct 12 I discovered earlier today via a post my sister put on Facebook that today would have been our mum's birthday! I posted Celine Dion's 'I Remember L.A.' in memory of her.

Whilst sat outside Café Délices having my usual latte, I observed a mother and daughter (daughter carrying young child). I noticed a material poppy'attached to the carrying yolk. Much respect and admiration to those three individuals.

Thurs 4th Oct 12 Touched base with BBC Guernsey. Left a copy of my poem 'See Me For Who I Am' for John Randall. I then nipped round to the Island FM studio to leave a copy of my poem with Mike Huston. Much thanks and appreciation for your valued time, Mike. Cheers aye, Gray.

Weds 10th Oct 12 Woke up feeling extremely exhausted! Came downstairs to the usual routine of being greeted by Bonnie and her usual morning, bracing K9 manner. Following my morning routine of coffee-cigarette and positive fix of Island FM with James Bentley and Claire Brouard I was greeted by Jenny. (I don't think she is much of a morning person – bless! LOL.)

I then went upstairs to get showered/shaved and bag packed for my boat-train trip to Aldershot in order to collect my suit medals, photos, veteran's badge and my valued collection of Runrig CDs. When I was sorted I took my bag downstairs to be greeted by Jenny pottering around in the kitchen. Jenny had been busy preparing David's lunch, at the same time she had made myself a couple of ham and mustard sarnies for the boat. Thanks Jenny – truly appreciated. I devoured them whilst on the Commodore Clipper on the overnight passage to Portsmouth. (My first ever voyage on board the Clipper was from Portsmouth to Guernsey in early 2003.) It was soon time to say cheerio to Jenny, David and Bonnie, prior to heading to the Clipper at four o'clock. My first task when I reached town (St Peter Port) was to go to Clinton Cards to buy a get-well card for Bill (who was in hospital). Bill, like myself, is a veteran, having served a 22-year career with the Royal Corps of Signals. Maximum respect and admiration to you, Bill. Cheers aye, Gray.

Thurs 11th Oct 12 On disembarkation in Portsmouth, I made my way to the train station in order to catch the train to Guildford so that I could catch the connecting train to

Aldershot. I phoned my mucker Miles whilst awaiting the train for the 'Shot'. He informed me that he would meet me off the train in the 'Shot'. In arrival in Aldershot, there was no sign of Miles! So I had a cigarette and waited patiently for his arrival. When he turned up, we took a walk into town so that Miles could get some essentials. We then got a taxi to Mike Jackson House. Once insid,e I had a good catch-up with Chris, Jo and Hazel. Jo, I will never forget the giant can of Stella or the time when I crashed out in the IT suite! 24918900 – Highlander Culton – Sir – laughing hysterically. Having had a good catch up with staff and Miles, and got my belongings, I said my goodbyes and made my way to Gatwick Airport in order to catch my flight back to Guernsey. During my flight back to paradise' (Glorious Guernsey) with Aurigny, I took some breathtaking photos on my mobile phone camera of cloud formations! They were truly heavenly images that I wanted to capture whilst I had the opportunity to.

Tues 16th Oct 12 Out with Bonnie this morning (down at Perelle) listening to 'Feel Good Tunes' and up to date Island info. Andy Newman DJing. I texted the studio to have a chance at the Daily Challenge! Ten minutes later my phone rang; on answering, Andy asked me if I would like to have a go at the Challenge. I responded with a positive 'Yes please'. Andy gave (offered) me two sets of questions (set 1 and 2). I opted for Set 1. I managed to answer four out of the eight questions correctly. (Someone by the name of Craig was the current champion, he managed to get his questions answered correctly – with some assistance from friends.) Well done Craig.

We as individuals have all got many choices to make in life! It is whether the choices we make as individuals are the right or wrong ones. Cheers aye, Gray.

FOR EVERY ACTION – THERE WILL ALWAYS BE A REACTION!

I messaged Dinger (Derek Bell) on Facebook to tell him about my book. Dinger was like a Big Brother figure to me when I joined the Queen's Own Highlanders in Dreghorn Barracks in '93. Dinger was the one responsible for getting me the nickname Nookie Bear.

Jenny dropped me off in town on her way to the hospital to see Bill. I will be going up to visit afterwards. On my way round to the Terminus Cafe I saw an old friend called Noel (BALL!), then I saw another friend, Dom. Was great catching up with them both. I then spotted Rob Moore (from Channel News – I remember Rob from his time working as a journalist/reporter with Island FM.) Rob was obviously on the tail of a great story! I say this as he was accompanied by a cameraman; the story they were following was related to the ice rink making a return to the market area. Much thanks and appreciation to all involved with the ice rink. You get a great view of Castle Cornet, as well as the marina from the bus terminus/café. Oh, can't forget the two phone boxes in their Guernsey yellow livery.

Weds 17th Oct 12 Woke up this morning to my routine of Island FM, coffee and cigarette. Then I went off to get my trainers (seeing as Bonnie wouldn't fetch them for me, LOL). Never stayed long at the beach due to there being a high tide. (So high the waves were slapping off the sea wall, thus creating spray across the road.)

Fri 19th Oct 12 After my usual wake-up routine of caffeine and nicotine and Island FM, I went on to the laptop. I woke early this morning (04:30) with a niggling feeling of the need to do something positive! I didn't know at the time of waking what that positive action was! I certainly knew the moment I logged into my Hotmail account and searched for Gill Shaw's Hotmail address.

I met Gill on two separate occasions (coincidentally both meetings occurred whilst in London). The first occasion was during a programme of 'Change' with registered charity Talking 2 Minds (massive thanks and appreciation to Rob Paxman – cheers aye, Gray). I met Gill in a lovely coffee shop near Grosvenor Square. I was truly honoured to meet your lovely self on that occasion, Gill. Much thanks and valued appreciation for my signed copy of *The Hero Inside.* (Officially authorised fundraising book for Help For Heroes.) The book was conceived and photographed by Gill. My second meeting with Gill was on Saturday 1st May 2010. Daz Hennesy and myself were sat on a wall across the road from Twickenham Stadium (half time during the Babcock Trophy Army vs Navy Rugby Match). Had a great chat with Gill telling her about the fundraising walk that we were to be undertaking with the registered charity Veterans-In-Action (VIA). Massive shout and thanks and appreciation to Billy Mcleod, Founder of VIA. Onwards and upwards, Billy. Cheers aye, Gray. The walk was one of many Union Flag Walks and would take the team from John O Groats all the way to Land's End. Gill kindly offered to take a couple of photos of Daz and I, prior to her heading off, and Daz and me going back in for the second half of the match.

The Royal Navy Team presented Billy with two rugby balls that day. I mentioned to Billy afterwards of the idea of carrying the balls throughout the walk as 'batons of hope' for other veterans, and so they were just that.

The walk took the month of May to complete, the team were pitching tents at various campsites throughout. From time to time, the team managed to get some fundraising days organised through various regional councils.

During one particular leg of the walk, I was paired up with an awesome guy by the name of Mark Smith. That leg of the walk involved walking across the Kessock Bridge (the same bridge that my loving mum brought an end to her years of trauma and anguish whilst living with her bipolar disorder). Mark was truly supportive and kept my spirits high and motivated. I truly forever appreciate and value your friendship/brotherhood, Mark. Kind and positive wishes to your awesome self and family. Onwards and upwards, bro. Cheers aye, Gray.

On reaching Inverness, I suggested to Mark about taking a slight detour and popping round to Inverness Caledonian Thistle Football Ground (on the off chance of meeting Terry Butcher). We never got to see Terry, although we did meet a lovely receptionist of the club. (My apologies for not remembering your name!) Thank you for your time and also for the two awesome signed panoramic photographs of Calies Ground. Cheers aye, Gray.

I remember one particular stage of the walk, where Billy and Ginge had gone to refuel the vehicles. Daz, Billy Jnr and Mark and myself stayed with the trailers in a lay-by at the side of a loch! Daz decided to go for a spot of hill/rock climbing (enough said for a former 'Royal' (Royal Marine)). LOL. We were honoured to have an RAF Hercules fly over the loch. We all showed our respect and appreciation to the Herc and crew. The pilot acknowledged us all by tilting the wings.

I found getting involved in VIA to be very beneficial to both my health and general well-being. Social integration is one of the positive, proactive characteristics of what the charity is about. Through my own involvement with VIA I have been out fundraising at the likes of Wembley, Twickenham, Stamford Bridge (Chelsea), Emirates (Arsenal), Ibrox (Rangers), Murrayfield (Edinburgh), Cardiff (Millennium Stadium), Manchester, Bristol, Carlisle, Newquay, Penzance, Portsmouth and Brighton to name but a few. I have also been involved in the Motorsport Endeavour Supacat day at Dunkeswell on Thursday 22nd July 2010. Much respect, thanks and valued appreciation to Jamie Clark and everyone involved in that very memorable day. Cheers aye, Gray. (I had an amazing experience driving a Jackal all-terrain vehicle with Billy riding shotgun in the back.) I have also been involved in several photography projects organised through Veterans-In-Action involving Mitsubishi, Pellier Noir. Much thanks and sincere appreciation to everyone involved in organising, planning and preparation of all of those truly amazing and very memorable experiences. Cheers aye, Gray. I was also involved in another VIA Union

Flag Walk from Land's End to Dover Castle. Another very memorable and positive experience, involving some truly awesome individuals/friends. I remember the massive deck chair near Bournemouth seafront!

I had a photo taken with the lovely Jo Cleary – thanks for sharing your green and white fizzy Haribo, Jo! (Just don't mention Haribo to 'Blue' (Carl Noble), as he goes funny with Haribo... LOL!) Thank you for your friendship Jo, of which I truly value and appreciate. Kind and forever best and positive wishes to you and family. Cheers aye, Gray. X

Now, on the subject of Blue! Blue is one of my favourite colours. Blue is also the name of an awesome boy band, much respect and admiration and thanks and appreciation to each and every member of the band. Cheers aye, Gray.

I remember taking Blaize to a music event at Sausmarez Park one year. Simon Webbe from Blue was performing that day. I managed to get Brian Dowling (from Big Brother), as well one of the former members of the boy band Busted, autographs to put in a book that I made for Blaize one year. Much thanks and appreciation to both. Cheers aye, Gray.

I remember my first admission to the Duchess of Kent's Psychiatric Hospital (Netley Ward) in 2002 (in Catterick). My at the time CPN (Community Psychiatric Nurse) – Captain Shuck – had decided to have me admitted following an incident on Waverley Bridge in Edinburgh. During my time on the ward I was downgraded as an infantry soldier (meaning I would never handle weapons again during the remainder of my Army career).

I was treated for depression and alcoholism during my time on Netley. I became good friends with other patients on the ward, one in particular was a guy by the name of Blue – Carl Noble. (Please don't mention HARIBO when Blue is around! (LMAO) Blue is very obsessed about his Haribo sweets – LOL (SELFISH)). I also befriended a guy by the name of Mark B whilst on the ward. Much thanks and appreciation to Mark and his mum for all they did for me during my times spent in Leeds. Cheers. Gray.

I also met a guy called Bryan (REME – Royal Electrical and Mechanical Engineers) and Colin (AGC – Adjutant General Corps). Much thanks and appreciation for your friendship and camaraderie. Gray.

Monday 10th June 2013

I am currently listening to 'Beneath Your Beautiful' (Labyrinth FEAT Emeli Sande) from Emeli's album 'Our Version of Events' (Special Edition). Emeli Sande and Labyrinth in my eyes and good ear (right) are truly amazing inspiration with their music magic. I first became aware of Emeli's lovely voice when I was employed as a Fire Marshal at the London 2012 Olympic/Paralympic Games. I will admit with positive ease that I am truly obsessed and inspired by so many musicians in the music industry/world. I am truly and sincerely grateful and appreciative to all in the industry.

I Graham Robert Culton would love to pay homage to the

following:

1) Runrig – Bruce Guthro, Calum and Rory Macdonald, Malcolm Jones, Iain Bayne, Brian Hurren, Donnie Munro (1974–1997), Pete Wishart (1986–2001), Mike Smith, Marlene Ross and all involved with Runrig. I have been a massive 'Riggie' from the age of 15, I have seen them in concert (twice) at Inverness Ice Rink 93/94 and also in Edinburgh at the Usher Hall in 2002. RUNRIG TRULY ROCK.

2) PINK and her dad, Jim Moore. Love and respect to you both. Gray x

3) Jessie J, Rihanna, Emeli Sande, Labyrinth, Nate Ruess, Christina Aguilera, Dido, Leona Lewis, Little Mix, Stooshe, Alicia Keys, Paloma Faith, Gabrielle Aplin, Lana Del Rey, Rumer, Robbie Williams, the Black Eyed Peas, Eva Cassidy, Train, Shakira, The Script, Take That, Demi Lovato, Miley Cyrus, Tina Turner, Celine Dion, Cyndi Lauper, Alison Moyet, Belinda Carlisle, Mica Paris, Sophie B Hawkins, Jon Secada, Savage Garden, The Tony Rich Project, Katie Melua, Kate Bush, Petula Clark, Natalie Imbruglia, Natasha Beddingfield, Annie Lennox, Dave Stewart, George Michael, Will Young, Boyzone, One Direction, David Bowie, David Gray, David Essex, Olly Murs, Sade, Kelly Clarkson x, Gary Barlow, Christina Perri, Anastacia, Fugees, Bono and U2, Beverley Knight, Beverley Craven, Bruce Springsteen (Boss), Nelly Furtado, James, James Morrison, Des'ree, Beyonce, Friday Hill, The Sterophonics, Dire Straits, Flo rida, Travie McCoy, The Notorious B.I.G., Puff Daddy, Trey Songz, Nicki Minaj and Crew, Coolio, Estelle, All-4-One, Color Me Badd, Gnarls

Barkley, Brandy, Sean Paul, Lil' Kim, Missy Elliot, Dawn Penn, K7, Dr Dre, House of Pain, Blazin' Squad, Cee Lo Green, En Vogue, Shola Ama, All Saints, Brand New Heavies, Craig David, Anita Baker, Mark Morrison, Alesha Dixon, Wiley, Keane, Bryan Adams, Kylie and Danni Minogue, Jason Donovan, The Carpenters, Red Hot Chilli Peppers, Red Hot Chilli Pipers, Pipes and Drums of the Queen's Own Highlanders/The Highlanders, Pipes and Drums of the Royal Scots Dragoon Guards, OMD, Lionel Richie, Blue, Sir Elton John, Daniel Beddingfield, David Sneddon, Travis, Sugababes, The Saturdays, Gabrielle, Barry White, Marvin Gaye, Bob Marley, Texas, Girls Aloud, Sir Tom Jones, Spice Girls, Mike and the Mechanics, Elvis (RIP), Merle Haggard, Samantha Mumba, The Farm, The LA's. R Kelly, Darius, The Police, Sting, Peter Cetera, Enrique Inglesias, Lulu, Ronan Keating, The Bee Gees, Marti Pellow, Wet Wet Wet, Gareth Gates, Billy Joel, Elvis Costello, Backstreet Boys, NSYNC, Westlife, Toni Braxton, Cher, Steps, K-CI + JoJo, Boyz II Men, Whitney Houston (RIP), Michael Jackson (RIP), Kenny G, The Military Wives and Gareth Malone, ELO, Daryl Hall/John Oates, The Steve Miller Band, Laura Brannigan, John Farnham, Toto, Dolly Parton, Kenny Rogers, Owen Paul, Dionne Warwick, Bill Medley and Jennifer Warnes, Wax, Roachford, The Maisonettes, Matthew Wilder, Boy Meets Girl, Hazel Dean, Mr Mister, Bangles, Bonnie Tyler, Deniece Williams, Irene Cara, Wham, Carly Simon, The Pointer Sisters, M, Fat Larry's Band, Kiki Dee, Bellamy Brothers, The Sutherland Brothers, Air Supply, Patrick Swayze (RIP), Wendy Fraser, Starship, Foreigner, Boston, Journey ('Don't Stop Believin''), the X-Factor Finalists 'Hero', Jean Michel Jarre, Prince, The

Soldiers, Clannad, Wolfstone, AKON, Newton Faulkner, Basshunter, The Shadows, Taylor Swift, Ed Sheeran, Daniel Merriweather, Ellie Goulding, Michael Bolton, LeAnn Rimes, Katherine Jenkins, Shakespeare's Sister, Eiffel 65, Britney Spears , Will.I.Am, Moloko, Diana Ross,Jamiroquai, The Cardigans, Supergrass, Phil Collins, Genesis, Honeyz, Martine McCutcheon, The Beatles, Ann Lee, Vengaboys, ATB, David Guetta, Alice Deejay, Tina Cousins, Aerosmith, ABBA, Coldplay, Paul Weller, The Stone Roses, Sir Andrew Lloyd Webber, Elaine Paige, Michael Crawford, Sarah Brightman, Dina Carroll, Marti Webb, Barbara Streisand, Sir Cliff Richard, Michael Ball, The Corrs, Michelle, Dame Kiri Te Kanawa, The Band of Her Majesty's Royal Marines, Lady Antebellum, DJ Sammy & Yanou (feat DO), Usher, The Calling, Atomic Kitten, Mary J Blige, Macy Gray, Hot Chocolate, M People, N Trance, DJ Kuta, Scooter, Shaggy, Cascada, R.E.M., D:Ream, East 17, Simply Red, Billy Idol, Happy Mondays, The B52's, The Rembrandts, Jimmy Sommerville, Limahl, Mr Big, Marc Cohn, The Levellers, The Commitments, Faith No More, Utah Saints, Armand Van Helden, Tori Amos, Dee-Lite, Whigfield, Corona, Gina G, JX, The Human League, Opus III, The Beloved, Snow, Peter Andre, Jimmy Nail, Muse, Michael Buble, Shontelle, James Arthur, Adele, Golden Earring, Fade to Gray (Visage) , The Wanted, Bros, Brother Beyond, Chris Malinchack, 10 Sharp, Amy Adams (Enchanted), Rita Ora, Naughty Boy, Bruno Mars, Justin Timberlake, Calvin Harris, Suggs, Madness, Billy Ocean, Boy George, Culture Club, Tiffany, Jessica Hammond, Kim Wilde, Tears for Fears, The Beat, Flock of Seagulls, Erasure, Pet Shop Boys, Split Endz, Guns'N'Roses, Fuzzbox, Strawberry Switchblade, Duffy,

Lady GaGa x, Dexy's Midnight Runners, The Manic Street Preachers, Hot Chocolate, Talking Heads, Nik Kershaw, Kenny Logan, Peter Gabriel, Lenny Kravitz, Adamski, Seal, Lonestar, The Fray, Journey South, The Beautiful South, Nickleback, Ben E King, Maria McKee, Labi Siffre, Ocean Colour Scene, JLS, Amelie, Huey Lewis and the News, The O'Jays, Anita Ward, Tracy Chapman, The Temptations, Kings of Leon, Pulp, Damon Albarn, Oasis, SNAP, Thompson Twins, Adam and the Ants, Shakin' Stevens, The Beach Boys, Van Morrison, Iron Maiden, Whitesnake, Alvin Stardust, Duran Duran, The Pretenders, OneRepublic, Lily Allen, Amy Winehouse (RIP x), Fun, The Killers, Brandon Flowers, BBE, Sasha, Grace Jones, Grace, Mansun, Faithless, PF Project feat Ewan McGregor, Olive, Robert Miles, Moby, DJ Jurgen, Darude, Fragma, Lasgo, DJ Quicksilver, Tiesto, Jurgen Vries, Milk Inc, Ian Van Dahl, Ferry Corsten, Howard Jones, Mark Brown feat Sarah Cracknel (The Journey Continues), Oakenfold, Armin Van Buuren, Tony de Vit, SIA, QFX, Q-Tex, Rod Stewart, The Rolling Stones, Big Country (RIP Stuart Adamson), Cascada, Crowded House, James Blunt (RESPECT SIR), Madonna, Goldie, Katrina and the Waves, Donna Lewis, The Family Stand, Shola Ama, Inner Circle. Big Mountain, Colour Me Badd, Hanson, The Brand New Heavies, The Beloved, Jose Gonzalez, Hurts, Mumford and Sons, Lighthouse Family, NEO, Jennifer Lopez x, Candy Dulfer, Eddie Reader, Taio Cruz, Disclosure feat Sam Smith, Kesha, Nicole Scherzinger, Bridgit Mendler, Avicii vs. Nicky Romero, Pitbull, Dizzee Rascal, Rudimental, Conor Maynard, The Lumineers (Ho Hey), Fleetwood Mac, The Justice Collective, Chicane, Jakatta, Plan B, Professor Green, The Feeling, Birdy,

Semisonic, Paulo Nutini, Scissor Sisters, Meatloaf, KT Tunstall, Goldfrapp, Athlete, Damien Rice, The Temper Trap, Eliza Doolittle, Corinne Bailey Rae, Norah Jones, Empire of the Sun, Rumer, Radiohead, Richard Ashcroft, Enigma, James Horner, Josh Groban, Robson and Jerome, Razorlight, Mika, Chumbawumba, No Doubt, Mathew Wilder, KC and the Sunshine Band, Fiction Factory, Living Joy, Owl City, Cybil, The Weather Girls, Ruffus, Backtreet Boys, 4 Non Blondes, Mariah Carey x, Monsters and Men, The Wonderstuff, Aztec Camera, Deacon Blue, Hothouse Flowers, Del Amitri, Jackie Wilson, Tanita Tikaram, Otis Reading, The Warrior Band (Heavy Souls), Chris De Burgh, The Commitments, The Cranberries, Sinitta, KLF, Tammy Wynette, Bette Midler, The Clash, The Cure, Sex Pistols, Ultravox, Marillion, Gary Moore (RIP), The Lightening Seeds, Pat Benatar, Gerry Rafferty, The Proclaimers (cheers aye Craig and Charlie), Patsy Cline (RIP), Simple Minds (Glittering Prize), Blondie, Eric Clapton, Billy Idol, Cutting Crew, Jimi Hendrix (RIP), Philip Oakley and Giorgio Moroder, Buzzcocks, EMF, Go West, It Bites, Stevie Wonder, Martha and the Muffins, Bryan Ferry and Roxy Music, Roxette, The Motors, The Dandy Warhols, The Skids, The Waterboys, The Stranglers, Glen Campbell, The Knack, Talk Talk, Thunder, The Quireboys, Poison, Ozzy Osbourne and Kelly Osbourne, Saxon, Tom Robinson Band, Andy Abraham, Don McLean, The Animals, Steve Harley and Cockney Rebel, Jan Hammer, Sacred Spirit (Yeha-Noha, wishes of happiness and prosperity), Celtic Woman, Youssou N'Dour, Neneh Cherry, MC Hammer, Jamie Cullum, Kinobe, Groove Armada, Reo Speedwagon, Carly Simon, Elkie Brooks, UB40, Luther Vandross, Busted, Passenger,

Kodaline, Mental as Anything, Europe, Candi Station, Stero MC's, Mark Owen, The GooGoo Dolls (Iris), Climie Fisher, Bruce Hornsby, Garth Brooks, Sister Sledge, Michael Bolton, Chicago, Ten City, Natalie Cole, Nick Kamen, Rick Astley, The Three Tenors, Berlin, Bonnie Tyler, Cher, Level 42, Bad Manners, Womack & Womack, Holly Johnson and Frankie Goes to Hollywood, Alannis Morisette, Bananarama, Communards, Then Jericho, Ben E King, Selena Gomez, Eminem, Snow Patrol, all musicians/artists and all associated with the music industry.

Sunday 18th November 2012 (Bella Luce Hotel, St Martins)

I went out for a cigarette, (listening to Marky T on Island FM). Conicidentally, Snow Patrol's 'Chasing Cars' was playing. This song has got so much meaning to me for many positive reasons.

Monday 19th November 2012

Following another restless sleep! I woke up before my alarm sounded. I had discussed with Lisa last night about getting myself out for a run in the morning. I endeavoured to get ready with the minimum of fuss so that I didn't disturb Lisa from her peaceful sleep.

Sat down for breakfast on my own (Lisa having a lie-in). Time for a positive moment of reflection and composure! I have never been much of a figure of composure in my past. I am gradually learning to do so with the support and friendship of Lisa. For your friendship and support Lisa Vallance, I am eternally grateful. Thank you, Now – Forever – Always. Gray xxx.

Tuesday 20th November 2012

Prior to heading out on my morning run, I took a moment of composure, with regards to how far I would go! I opted to head towards the Co-op (St Martins) then on to St Martin's Village and out towards the Wicked Wolf. Once here, I decided to head back to the village, down the lane past the school and arriving back at the Bella Luce.

Thursday 25th October 2012

Awoke at 06:30. Blaize and Tatnall residence were all still asleep, that is all except for Bonnie who was eagerly awaiting her early morning scurry on the beach at Perelle. On return to the house, Blaize was awake and waiting to see Bonnie. Sorted Blaize out with breakfast, I then went to the back garden to do some burning for Bill. Time was getting on! So I made sure the rubbish in the incinerator was not likely to spread and went up to get showered and booted and suited prior to heading into town for the 2012 Poppy Appeal Service of Dedication at the War Memorial at the top of Smith Street (St Peter Port). Whilst walking up hill to the mMonument, had a chat with the lovely WPC Lisa McMillan. Blaize and Lisa were doing high 6s with each other! When at the monument, I had a brief catch-up with John Brehaut. I then had a catch-up with Bob Plaice. Those veterans and dignitaries and representatives from various associations/organisations that were laying crosses of remembrance began to form up in front of the War Memorial in readiness for the Dean of Guernsey commencing the service. A cannon blast from Castle Cornet signalled noon, and the Dean commenced the service. Following the brilliant service, the laying of crosses began. It wasn't long before Blaize and I were making our way up the few steps; I had decided to allow Blaize to lay her first cross herself. When she had finished her good deed, she took a step back, paused, before saying "Thank you". At that moment I removed my Glengarry and paid homage to our fallen. I then replaced my Glengarry back on head, and Blaize and I took up position with the rest of the parade. I felt overwhelmingly proud of Blaize following her laying her first ever cross of remembrance. That is not to say that I am proud to be her dad 24/7.

The cross that Blaize had placed had the British Army logo on it.

The cross also had the names of Fusilier Gordon Gentle – 1 Royal Highland Fusiliers – and Guardsman Jamie Janes – Grenadier Guards. When the service was over I got chatting to a photographer from the Guernsey Press followed by a lovely lady from Channel Report.

My first ever experience of Guernsey came about in 1996, following the passing of my mum. Following her funeral and my return back to the Battalion in Ebrington Barracks, it was decided by hierarchy that I would benefit from some time out away from the province. And so I was sent on a Joint Sailing Expedition. I met up with the rest of the crew in Portsmouth. On leaving Pompey we set sail westward, following the coast to Cornwall. Both the skipper and 2nd Mate had military experience (Royal Navy/Marines). RESPECT. The rest of the crew were made up of trainees from various corps of the Army. Respect to them.

The plan of action for the expedition was to give the crew a hands-on experience of sailing. After time spent down on the Cornish coast, we made our course across the Channel to Glorious Guernsey – St Peter Port. It was here that I had my first ever experience and breathtaking sights on Guernsey soil. We had a stopover night, thus enabling the crew to sample the nightlife of St Peter Port. On that night I ventured into the Ship and Crown pub. I discovered in 2003 the landlord of the pub was a gentleman fellow veteran by the name of Mark Pontin. Coincidentally, Mark is still landlord (an awesome one at that) of the pub.

Following my great experience in Glorious Guernsey, the crew and myself made passage for Alderney'(Aurigny) where we had the opportunity to sample some of the island life (pubs) there. When we left Alderney the following day (with minor hangovers LOL), we made passage back to Portsmouth.

On arrival back at base, we all mucked in to ensure that the yacht was ready for her next voyage/expedition.

I said my thanks and appreciation to the crew and made my way back to London in order to catch my flight back to Belfast.

"WHAT WE DO IN LIFE... ECHOES IN ETERNITY."
(quality quote from the award-winning movie *GLADIATOR*)

“I SOMETIMES FEEL LIKE I AM DIAGONALLY PARKED IN A PARALLEL UNIVERSE!” (AUTHOR UNKNOWN)

“FOR EVERY ACTION IN YOUR LIFE! A REACTION WILL BE SURE TO FOLLOW! (EVERY ACTION BARES A CONSEQUENCE! BE SURE THINGS YOU DO TODAY ARE WORTH THE PRICE YOU PAY TOMORROW!” (AUTHOR UNKNOWN).

OUR YOUNGER GENERATION OF TODAY… ARE OUR FUTURE FOR TOMORROW. (They do not ask to be brought into a world of HATE, ANIMOSITY, HOSTILITY, NEGATIVE EVENTS.)

For the last 38 years of my life, I have lived through severe adversity. At the same time I have adopted various coping strategies! In the last six months I have realised/discovered that there was obviously not a great deal of understanding and awareness of autism when I was born in 1975!

My difficult upbringing from childhood enhanced the symptoms of my health (psychological conditions that I am living with today.) My underlying and undiagnosed autism has enhanced my adverse well-being lifestyle, and through myself being unaware of being autistic, other individuals who have been associated with me have also been unaware.

I am not aware of any difficulties encountered at birth, I am however aware of many cases/experiences of head trauma from childhood. I have also been a victim of abuse from childhood from psychological, mental, physical, verbal and one case of domestic abuse. I have witnessed extreme levels of genocide, animosity, hostility and conflict.

Through development of overlapping personal health issues, and many traumatic experiences – heartache, sorrow, grief, bereavement from loss of loved ones and great friends – my psychological defences have been enhanced to a high degree of self-preservation (protection). Since my medical discharge from the British Army in January 2003, I have been gradually believing that I have been living with the symptoms of combat-related post-traumatic stress disorder, following my regular service with the Queen's Own Highlanders/ Highlanders. Whereas the reality and truth of my prolonged suffering in silence has been down to a multitude of complex issues/events/experiences in my life to date.

My symptoms of PTSD have been offset by my autism, my well-being issues in life (negative) have had a detrimental knock-on effect during my recovery and development in life.

My past life is exactly just that – I am no longer held back in my recovery and development in life in my onwards and upwards positive journey of life.

I have truly and genuinely learned from my mistakes made in the past, and I am now going to endeavour to continue my life journey with a more positive and proactive and professional manner, with an awesome sense of POSITIVE PANACHE (confident and stylish manner).

My own PPPOA (Personal, Positive Plan of Action) for the future is as follows... To live MY life in positive peace and harmony and passion for music and humour.

I intend to work in UNISON with medical professionals and agencies/organisations unhindered by negativity.

I plan on undertaking a degree in Psychotherapy in 2014.

Cheers aye.
Graham Robert Culton

Courage and Strength – Strength and Honour

ONWARDS AND UPWARDS

Gray.

Positive Proactive Action

Everybody has a soul desire to succeed in life.
Nobody requires anguish, adversity, times of strife!
Stereotypical comments… regards gender, religion, culture, and race… will continue to create a negative mindset of societal disgrace!
We are all individuals in life, with similar needs, and varying creeds!
A great well-being, stability, protection, desire to be loved and accepted.
Much misunderstandings, ignorance, arrogance and misconception create feelings of isolation, worthlessness, negativity and rejection.
My many moments of positive composure have given me time to reflect! Thus resolving my confusion of much and feelings of disrespect.
NLP may not be everyone's cup of tea!
One positive trait for sure… it certainly is for me.
What is now left to say? Other than wish you all a 'GrayT Day'… with positive proactive actions all the way.

Positive Proctive Action.
G. Culton (20th September 2014).